Mandy
The Mischievous Elf

Written by Bill Dale Grizzle
Illustrated by Carlos Lemos

ISBN 978-1-61225-278-0

Published by Mirror Publishing
Milwaukee, WI 53214
www.pagesofwonder.com

Printed in the USA.

For Mallory,
my biggest fan

Thank you, Amanda,
for inspiring this story

Many thanks to my dear friend and editor, Rhonda Hicks Willis,
for her hours of labor on this story, and others.

Part One
A Case of Mischiefitus

Chapter One

Rocco Roundrock was nervous. He really didn't know why. He'd never seen the big guy angry, or even raise his voice at anyone for that matter. He always handled problems at the shops and toy factories with patience and understanding. But still, he'd only been in his current position for a few short years, and having to report an incident to the main office was a little nerve-racking.

"Uh, Santa, I really don't know how this happened. They just started coming down the assembly line like that." Santa looked up at Rocco and grunted before turning the toy fire truck over in his hands once more.

"Well, this will never do." Santa's soft chuckle caught Rocco by surprise as he watched the smiling old fellow spin the square wheels of the truck. "How many did we make with square wheels?" he asked.

"Two hundred and seventy-three," replied Rocco, rather shyly. "Thankfully, Hoppy and his crew caught it before the whole batch was ruined. I'm really sorry, Santa."

"It's not your fault, Rocco," said Santa as he stood to walk around his big desk. "I'm just glad it wasn't like the last time. The last time this happened the doll factory made more than seventeen hundred dolls that sounded like goats when they were supposed to be saying 'mommy'." Santa sat down on a sofa and motioned for Rocco to sit beside him. "Yep, I've been expecting this any day now, so I'm not totally surprised."

Just as Rocco was about to ask Santa what he meant, there was a sharp rap at the door, and then it flew open.

"Santa, Rocco," it was Hollie Hoxlee, Rocco's assistant, out of breath and obviously very upset. "We have problems *everywhere*," she cried. "At the ball factory, the footballs are perfectly round and the basketballs are shaped like footballs." Her already bulging eyes became even larger as she pointed at the fire truck in Santa's hands. "And the soccer balls are square like those wheels!" Hollie managed to catch a deep breath before she continued. "And at the doll factory, Tiny Tina is coming out with her legs where her arms are supposed to be and her arms where her legs go. *They look disgusting!* We have a whole shipment of snow sleds with the runners on backwards, the yo-yos won't crawl back up their strings, the tops won't spin, and you don't *even* want to know what the jack-in-the-boxes are doing. I didn't know what else to do, so I just shut the whole factory down." With that, Hollie collapsed into the nearest chair, covered her face with her hands and moaned.

"Now, now, Hollie," said Santa softly as he placed a gentle hand on the top of her head. "You did exactly what you were supposed to do. However, we must fix these problems and keep our eyes open for others that may come along. Hollie, send all the defective toys to the repair shop; tell them to recycle these square wheels into building blocks," he added as he handed her the fire truck. "Have them repair and reshape everything; they'll be as good as new. Tell Buttons Bailey at the repair shop to call me if there are any questions. Now be on your way my little Elf, it's too near the Christmas season to be shut down for very long."

Rocco marveled at the kindness in Santa's voice; his jolly nature, as if nothing really mattered, almost as if nothing really concerned him. But he knew for sure that was really not the case.

"We must devise a plan to catch her in the act, Rocco," said Santa.

"Her?" questioned Rocco. "And what did you mean when you said you had been expecting this?"

"Yes," answered Santa, "her. Our culprit is a girl Elf; it's always a girl. And this is not the first time this kind of thing has happened. Down through the ages there have been two Elf families afflicted by a condition known as mischiefitus. It causes one to engage in unusual and quite often mischievous behavior. Then there are cases like this, the more severe cases, where their behavior is, might we say, disruptive. It's genetic, Rocco...."

"Gen, who?" interrupted Rocco, his eyes wide open with curiosity.

"Genetic, Rocco, which means that she was born with it. It affects the third daughter of a third daughter.....oh never mind. She can't help herself, Rocco, in fact she has no idea she's done anything wrong. Mischiefitus is passed from one generation to the next, but only the girl Elves are affected. Well, except for once."

Santa stood and began pacing the floor with a worried look on his face that Rocco had never seen before. He paced back and forth; he rubbed his head; he rubbed his chin, and he thought deeply. Finally, he reclaimed his seat on the couch beside Rocco.

"Rocco," he began, "you have been made superintendent of all the Elves because you've earned it. You have proven yourself capable and trustworthy. You are my right-hand man as well as my friend, therefore it is time for you to know the whole story." Santa took a deep breath and let it out slowly, then he began.

"Several generations ago, long before your time, Rocco, there was a boy Elf named Evail Elderberry. He seemed to be an ordinary boy, just like a dozen other young Elves born about that time. He romped in the snow and played and had a grand time; frankly, I had high hopes for the boy. What I didn't realize, though, was that through some oddity of nature, Evail had been born with mischiefitus; and when it came out, as it always does, it came out with a great fury. We were in turmoil for two full Christmas seasons before I finally caught him in the act."

Santa slowly shook his head, and Rocco could plainly see that the usual twinkle in his eyes had been clouded over by a deep hurt. This was a difficult subject for the big guy, and Rocco knew it.

"We had always been able to cure mischiefitus with treatments of proper discipline and large doses of love and compassion, but Evail was different. I suppose being a boy may have had something to do with it, but he did not respond to treatment at all. If anything, it just made matters worse. For many seasons, I tried everything in the books to cure Evail with absolutely no success.

He even changed his name, and started calling himself Elf Evil."

These last words struck Rocco's ears with a jolt. His whole life he had heard rumors of an evil Elf sometime back in ancient history, but this was concrete evidence that such an Elf existed. This was coming from the big man himself, Santa Claus.

"Wha....what happened to Evail, Santa?" was Rocco's meek reply.

"The worst fate that could befall an Elf," answered Santa, "and it breaks my heart to this very day. A high court of Elves was convened and Evail was found to be guilty of a thousand charges. The court recommended that he be banished from the kingdom. So, after one final plea from me that he mend his ways, Evail refused and showed no remorse while doing so. Simply stated, he was not sorry for anything he had done. So, with a heavy heart, I banished Evail Elderberry from the Kingdom of Claus forever and sent him to the South Pole. To add to my distress, utilizing his gift of gab he convinced his entire family and some of their closest friends to go with him. Evail has never returned to the North Pole, and as far as I know, he has not turned from his wicked ways. But I still have hope in my heart that he will someday."

Santa Claus fell silent for a long while; his thoughts far back in time. Then suddenly, he jumped to his feet. "Come, Rocco, we must put our plan into action. I'm pretty sure I know who the culprit is, but we must set a trap. I will announce that we have a special order for a few hundred gum ball machines, and also a special order for a shipment of marbles. She'll not be able to resist the temptation to switch the marbles with the gum balls. I'll catch her in the act!"

Later that morning Santa announced the special order request and the plan was put into motion. That very night, just after midnight, and well hidden among cartons and crates, Santa watched as Elf Mandy Mayflower emptied a bag of marbles into the gum ball loading machine. She was caught in the act.

Chapter Two

Early the next morning Elf Mandy Mayflower was escorted to the office of Santa Claus, where she was deposited at his desk.

"Mandy."

"Yes, Santa," she giggled, and allowed her eyes to gaze around the boss's office; a place she had never been until now.

"Did you put marbles into the gum ball loading machine last night?" asked Santa as he tried to keep a straight face; realizing that Mandy had no idea that she was in trouble for what she had done made the situation a little comical.

"Yes, Santa," she giggled again. "And I also put gum balls in with the marbles."

"Did you also make some adjustments to the yo-yo and top machines?"

"Yes, Santa, and that's not all. The pogo sticks are awesome now."

This prompted Santa to make a quick call to the pogo stick department. Shaking his head he asked, "why?"

"I just felt like it, and besides it's funny; everybody thinks it's funny."

Santa let out a sigh. "Then will you please tell me how you reprogrammed the fire truck, doll, and jack-in-the-box machines?"

"Yes, Santa," this time her giggle was a laugh. "With these." Mandy reached into her pocket and pulled out a handful of little plastic gadgets. "I just plug them into the computers and.....done."

Santa held out his hand and Mandy dropped six computer flash drives into it. Suddenly Santa was struck with the realization that this problem might be even more serious than he'd thought.

"Where did you get these, Mandy?"

"From Tripper, he gave them to me and told me what to do with them."

"Who is Tripper?" asked Santa. "I don't recall having heard that name before."

"Oh, he's my new friend who moved here a couple of seasons ago. Tripper doesn't have a family; he stays in the storage shed behind the cookie shop and is only friends with me and my cousins."

"Oh, really. Do you have any more of these things?" Santa cringed at the answer that came.

"Yes, Santa, lots of them."

Santa really dreaded the answer to the next question that had to be asked. "How many have you plugged into computers?"

"All of them, Santa, all of them." Mandy was as happy as a lark, completely unaware that she was under the spell of mischiefitus.

The jolly old man was not so jolly as he lowered his head into his hands and muttered, "Oh my goodness; what damages have been done?"

By the end of the day Santa and Rocco along with a half-dozen trusty Elves had gathered all the flash drives, checked all of the computer systems at all of the different toy factories and shops, and made the necessary repairs. Their final stop of the day was at the shed behind the cookie shop. Santa was not surprised to find no trace of Elf Tripper. In fact, it appeared as though he had been gone for some days now.

"I fear that Elf Tripper, if that is actually his real name, may be a member of Evail Elderberry's family," Santa whispered to Rocco in confidence. "I have always had a fear that he would find a way to make things difficult for us. He may have found a way to slip one of his relatives in here; and even worse, he may have devised a way to disrupt our computer systems. I would like to believe that Mandy becoming involved was simply a coincidence, but if Tripper has been here for two seasons and was only friends with her and her cousins that may not be the case. Evail may have figured out when her mischiefitus might surface and was watching and waiting. The ideal way to create chaos is from within. Am I not correct, Rocco?"

"Yes, Santa," answered Rocco, "I think you may be absolutely right about everything, but we've checked all the computers and fixed everything that we found wrong."

"This is true, my friend, but still we must stay alert for the aggravations that have not yet shown themselves. Blasted computers; I didn't like the first one, and I still don't like them."

Rocco lowered his eyes and allowed Santa some room to vent his frustrations. "I know how you feel about them, Santa, but I don't know how we could do without them now. It's a different time, you know. We have to keep up with the times."

Santa only grunted. "Right now there is the matter of Mandy Mayflower that I must deal with....first thing in the morning."

Chapter Three

Santa Claus was mulling over reports that the Elf supervisors had prepared the evening before. The reports concerned the damages and corrective actions that had been taken to solve the problems that Mandy Mayflower had caused when she entered his office.

"You wanted to see me again, Santa?" Mandy was as cheerful and upbeat as an Elf could be; not one hint of dread was in her voice.

Peering over his glasses and the paper he held in his hand, Santa sighed and shook his head from side to side. "Mandy, you don't have a clue that you're in trouble, do you?"

"Mother said I was, but I don't know why. I haven't done anything wrong."

"Did your mother explain to you what's going on," asked Santa, "inside of you, I mean? Did she explain to you about your....condition?"

"Yes, Santa," she giggled and bounced around paying little attention to the big man across the desk from her.

"Well," said Santa, "what did your mother tell you?"

"She said that I have mischiefitus or something like that. She said that I have done a bunch of bad things and have caused a lot of trouble for you. But Santa, I don't feel like I've done bad things. I've just done funny things; everybody thinks it's funny."

"No Mandy," Santa said softly, "not everybody thinks it's funny. In fact only you can see any humor in what you've done."

The little Elf simply stared at Santa. For the life of her she could not understand why he would not see that *everything* was funny.

"Regrettably," Santa continued in his usual soft voice, "this is what must be done. The treatment for mischiefitus is proper discipline, along with large amounts of love and compassion. Therefore, you will be assigned a new job; you will not be allowed in the doll factory nor will you be allowed in any of the factories or shops for as long as it takes for you to be cured. Your job from now until you're free of this condition will be to care for the Genpuni. You are to feed them seven times a day and make sure that their hutches are clean at all times. Another part of your punishment will be that you write a weekly report on your job at the hutches....in longhand."

"The birds!" squealed Mandy. "Why the birds? I don't like the Genpuni; they'll peck you on the fingers. I don't even know why you still keep them anyway; you don't use their feathers as pens anymore. You write all of your letters on a computer, don't you?"

This may be progress already, thought Santa, because it was the first emotion he'd seen out of Mandy besides utter happiness and bliss in two days. "I keep the Genpuni because of my love for them and the fact that they have a place here, as much a place as you, young lady. Besides, you never know when you might need a good pen. Now off with you. Paddy, the regular Genpuni caretaker, is waiting right outside; he will show you how to do everything. I'll look for your first report one week from today."

Santa held on to the stern expression he wore on his face until Mandy was out of his office. He hated to be so severe with the girl, yet he knew he must to keep her on a path to recovery. "Please let her healing come quickly," his prayer was whispered before he fell silent and slipped into deep thought concerning the computer problems that had popped up during the night.

Chapter Four

The first week went by, along with Mandy's first report, then the second and third. She was miserable. She had grown up in a family of doll makers; she was proud of her heritage, but now she'd been reduced to gathering fallen feathers.

To make matters worse, she had sore fingers because she had not learned how to scatter their seed fast enough to avoid the Genpuni's hungry pecks.

"You bunch of bad birds!" she screamed. "I dislike you more and more every day."

"Have patience, dear one," said old Paddy. "You will learn to love them some day."

"*What...ever*," she mumbled as she slammed shut the door of the hutch. Love these nasty birds, she thought, I don't think so! "I'm finished for today." She carelessly threw her words over her shoulder in Paddy's direction and then left. Once outside, Mandy found a quiet spot beneath a giant evergreen with low hanging limbs. She settled down onto a blanket of fresh snow and gazed at the approaching nightfall. The weight of the world seemed to rest on her tiny shoulders, and she felt completely overwhelmed with sadness. Then Mandy Mayflower did an unusual thing, a very unusual thing indeed for an Elf: she cried from a broken heart.

"Is this all there is for me now?" she sobbed as she watched the twinkling of the first star of the evening. "Is this all there is...?"

Mandy's healing, though far from complete, had at last begun.

Part Two
Santa's Pens

Chapter Five

Santa Claus sat quietly behind his desk with a stack of reports before him outlining the dozens of problems the various toy factories and shops were experiencing. On the opposite side of his desk, three anxious Elf supervisors shifted their weight from one foot to the other while waiting for a response from the big guy.

Finally, Penny Pulmbob broke the silence. "What are we going to do, Santa? Practically every computer system in the entire kingdom has been affected in some way or another. *Every* factory and *all* the shops are behind schedule."

"That's the truth," added Jack Jumpingjack, "at this rate, the Christmas season will be here and we won't have enough toy trucks to fill half our orders. Why, Rocco and the computer guys are over there now trying to fix things. What *are* we going to do?"

"Hold on there, Elves," said Santa, raising his hands above his head. "Everything will be okay; we'll figure all this out, but we can't allow ourselves to get too excited. We must work together to solve these problems. And don't worry Jack, there *will* be enough trucks; there's always enough trucks." Santa couldn't help but notice the doubtful look on all three faces staring at him. "Now why don't you all go home; it's late in the day and you need to get some rest. Tomorrow morning will come early."

The three Elves left Santa still seated behind his desk. What they didn't know was that Santa really didn't know how he was going to fix all the problems they were facing. Nor did the Elves know that things were much worse than they realized.

For the past three weeks it seemed as though everything that could go wrong had gone wrong, and Santa knew that it all stemmed from those pesky little flash drives that Mandy Mayflower had plugged into the computers. He also knew that it would be very difficult to fix everything, if indeed they could be fixed. To add to his dismay, Mandy, the main computer operator at the doll factory, who would be a great asset to the repair efforts, had shown absolutely no sign of improvement. He picked up the job report she had turned in the day before; her third report read almost exactly like her second report, as well as her first. They were filled with harsh words of unhappiness, dislike for the Genpuni, and complaints about her sore fingers. His glimmer of hope that she would quickly recover from her case of mischiefitus was just that, a glimmer.

Santa leaned back in his big chair, closed his eyes, and again whispered a prayer for his wayward Elf; a prayer in fact for all his hardworking Elves, and all the children of the world who would be counting on them during the upcoming Christmas season. Soon the big guy was lost in thoughts of happier times.

"I must go home," he exclaimed aloud and sprang to his feet. "Mrs. Claus will be wondering what has happened to me, and my supper will surely be cold by now." Santa scampered out of his office and toward his cozy cottage where the smells of warm, homemade bread and steaming hot soup greeted him at the door.

"I was beginning to worry about you," shrieked Mrs. Claus as she rushed to help her husband out of his coat. "It's so bitterly cold outside tonight, and you're not properly dressed to be wandering about, you know."

"Oh, don't worry so my dear." Santa gently patted her cheeks between both of his big hands, "I was not out wandering about. I have been at my office all evening working on these problems."

"Any progress?" she asked as she hung his heavy coat on a sturdy hook just inside the little coat closet.

"Maybe, some. They're like snow drifts; they just keep piling up. We fix a few and before we know it, others have taken their place." Santa shook his head and stared at the floor. "We've a long way to go, Missis, and there's no telling what tomorrow may bring."

"Well, tomorrow is tomorrow," Mrs. Claus cheerfully stated, "so for tonight, let's get you some supper and then a good night's rest."

Santa just smiled, thankful in his heart for the love he felt.

Chapter Six

"Nicklaus!" Santa's pleasant dreams and restful sleep were rudely interrupted by the shriek of Mrs. Claus's voice. "Nicklaus! Someone is pounding on the door. Nicklaus!" Mrs. Claus usually called him Nick. Only when she was excited did she call him Nicklaus.

Santa finally collected his senses, stumbled from the warm, cozy bed, slipped on his house shoes and made his way to the door.

"Santa." The late night visitor was, Kimmie Kiddermore, a search and rescue officer. "Sorry to have to disturb you at this late hour, but we have an emergency situation that you need to be aware of."

"Yes," said Santa. At once thoughts of something terrible happening at one of the toy factories ran through his head.

"Mandy Mayflower is in the hospital," the officer reported. "She didn't make it home after she left work, and after a couple of hours her family became concerned and contacted search and rescue. We found her about an hour ago huddled beneath one of the giant evergreen trees in Christmas Park. Santa, she was unconscious and almost frozen."

This news struck Santa very hard, and within minutes he was dressed to go to the hospital. "Elizabeth, fetch me my heavy robe, will you please? I believe it's a night suitable for a warmer garment." He kissed his wife on the cheek as he started for the door. "Say a prayer for that little Elf; she needs our prayers."

Fifteen minutes later, Santa was seated beside Mandy's hospital bed. She was still unconscious, but the nurse reported that her temperature had almost returned to normal and that she should be okay. Santa studied the face of his young Elf, wondering how she had gotten herself into such a predicament. Soon, in the quietness of the hospital room and with a prayer in his mind, he fell asleep with his hand resting on the forearm of the hapless little Elf.

Hapless indeed, for she had been born the third daughter of a third daughter of a third daughter, to the only remaining Elf family at the North Pole to be plagued with the mischiefitus gene.

Sometime before daybreak Santa was awakened by the movement of Mandy's arm. She then removed his hand from her arm and moved it out of his reach. She glared at him with a harsh expression as he spoke softly.

"You gave us quite a scare, young lady. We're so thankful that you're okay."

"What are you doing here?" she snapped. "Why should you care? Where am I anyway? How did I get here?"

Santa explained what had happened as best he could, since he really didn't know why she had not gone straight home on such a bitterly cold night.

"Well, it's your fault!" she snapped again. "It's *all* your fault! If you hadn't sent me to take care of those miserable birds this would not have happened. I want you to leave now, and I don't ever want to see you again!"

"I know you're unhappy now, Mandy, but please try to understand that this is all for your welfare. I know that the Genpuni can be aggravating at times, but if you will pay attention to what Paddy is trying to teach you, just maybe everything will be soon be back to normal again."

"Welfare!" Mandy screamed. "You call almost freezing, *welfare?*" At this point she turned her back to Santa. "Just go away, I don't need you."

Once again Mandy moved her arm to avoid Santa's touch, and with a heart heavier than it had been since the days of Evail Elderberry, he slowly left the room.

Chapter Seven

Three days later Mandy was back at work tending to the Genpuni, only now she was angrier than before. Now she was bitter, and her mind dwelt on ways of getting even with the Genpuni and Santa Claus.

Out of concern Paddy reported to Santa, "I am worried about her, boss. She is so angry I fear that she will do something really bad. I know that this is all part of her healing; that anger always follows happiness and bliss, but still I worry."

"As do I, Paddy." The wise old Elf was comforted by Santa's calm words. "Just keep an eye on her, and hope and pray that she makes it through this stage without causing too much commotion."

"I'll do my best," said Paddy, as he shook Santa's hand and left.

However, in a short while he was back and out of breath from rushing as fast as he could all the way from the Genpuni hutches.

"When I got back," he gasped, "Mandy Mayflower was sitting beside the fireplace in my office with a cup of hot chocolate, and *every* hutch was open and *every* Genpuni was gone. I was afraid of this, Santa."

Santa and Paddy hurried back to the hutches, where sure enough they found Mandy still enjoying her hot chocolate beside the warm fire.

"What is the meaning of this, Mandy Mayflower, you know that the Genpuni are not used to being in the wild. They can't possibly survive out there." Santa tried his best to sound angry, but at best he was sure she saw that he was more annoyed than angry. The Genpuni had escaped many times down through the decades, but they always came home. Santa was sure that from time to time they enjoyed some leisure time to fly outside of the boundaries of their hutches; to soar on the winds and frolic in the snow. He was not overly concerned about the birds; he was, however, concerned about Mandy's behavior.

"They wanted out," the sharpness of her reply pricked Santa's heart. "So knowing how it feels to be trapped where you don't want to be, I let them out."

"You are not the wise old soul that you think yourself to be, young lady," said Santa. "So while they are out for a little exercise you can take advantage of their absence and give their hutches an extra good cleaning. They'll be back at sunset so be ready for them. And don't leave until all of them are back safely in their hutch."

"You mean they're coming back.....all by themselves?" Mandy could not believe what she was hearing. She thought for sure that they would be gone forever. "Why?" she asked.

"They live here, Mandy, just like you do," Santa's voice softened. "And as I told you before, they belong here, just like you do. Everyone and every creature here has its own place in the delicate balance of the Kingdom of Claus. Everything that we do has an effect on someone or something. But what we don't know is how far into the future that effect may last. Therefore, it is always advisable that our actions be positive and good so that the effect may also be positive and good." Santa shrugged his shoulders and took a deep breath. "But, there again, our Creator gave us free will and the option to make our own choices. In this case, you chose to let the Genpuni out just because *you* are unhappy about being here. So it's really up to us as to how we affect others, isn't it? Consider what might happen to those poor birds if they didn't know to come back. Think about that, and report to me about the condition of the Genpuni in the morning."

With that, Santa left.

"You heard the boss, Mandy, so busy yourself; you've a lot to do before sunset." Now Paddy was gone, leaving Mandy alone with her thoughts and a lot of cleaning to do.

Sure enough, just before sunset the Genpuni began to return. At first one by one, then by two's and three's, and then by small flocks. Each bird went to its own hutch as if this was an everyday occurrence. By dark all the Genpuni were safely back in their hutches, all except one. Mandy fed the birds and closed their hutch doors, but none of them ate with their usual eagerness.

Instead, they stood in silence and looked in the direction of the empty hutch. Mandy watched in amazement as not one single bird partook of its seed nor did any of them make their usual cooing sounds. It occurred to her that they were acting out of concern for their missing companion.

"Wow," she said softly, "they're worried about the missing one. I didn't realize that they could have feelings like that." Mandy rushed to the window and scanned the horizon for the missing bird. Nothing. She whistled and called for the Genpuni for a long while. Still nothing. Suddenly her heart was heavier than she ever thought possible; even heavier than the evening under the evergreen tree when she cried herself to sleep and almost froze. But this time she didn't cry; this time she thought clearly, and she knew what she had to do. She had to find the missing bird. So slipping into the warmest boots she could find in the storage room and throwing on the heaviest robe, she went out into the howling wind and flying snow of the night.

Mandy searched everywhere she could think of: every tree, every shed, every barn. Then she searched further from the village. The little Elf struggled through the deep snow, sometimes walking against the vicious and piercing winds; all the time whistling and calling for the lost bird. Mandy searched for hours to no avail, but she would not give up. Without realizing it, she became weaker and weaker from the cold; the bitter cold that was draining her of her strength and her ability to think clearly. Before long she was in as much danger as the Genpuni she was searching for.

Meanwhile, back at the hutches, the Genpuni were becoming more and more restless and a deeper-than-usual cooing was beginning to rumble among them. Their concern for their fellow bird now included their keeper. Suddenly, one of the more mature birds began to peck at the latch of her hutch, and soon it opened. Others followed suit, and before long all the Genpuni were out of their hutches again. They cooed, flapped their oversized wings, bobbed their heads, and then they flew out into the darkness. They circled the village, they circled the kingdom and they found no trace of their companion, but they did find their keeper. There she was, a very long way from the village, huddled against an overturned and abandoned snow sleigh. Mandy marveled as the entire flock gathered closely around her, spreading their wings to shield her from the howling wind. Then happy cooing resounded through the flock as she slowly opened her robe just far enough to reveal the missing Genpuni, wrapped snugly in her arms.

Early the next morning the search and rescue unit once again found Mandy Mayflower asleep in the snow. Only this time she was safe and warm, surrounded by the flock of Genpuni who had used their bodies to keep the Elf girl as warm as if she had been at home in her own bed.

"Santa," said Mikey Micklehorn, the chief of search and rescue, "I've never seen anything like this. It's a miracle for sure. The Genpuni kept that girl alive by keeping her warm."

"Miracle," answered Santa in a quiet voice, "maybe; but I'm more likely to believe that it was a coming to an understanding. And I think we will find that Mandy Mayflower is well on her way to being cured of her mischiefitus."

"Santa," exclaimed Mandy, "I'm fine and I'm ready to go back to work. The Genpuni need me; they're waiting for me." Mandy jumped from the exam table in the hospital emergency room. "I'm sorry for all those mean things I said to you the other day, Santa. May I go now? Really, I'm fine."

The nurse nodded, and Mandy was gone in a flash.

Later that day Santa stopped by the Genpuni hutches. He smiled as he watched Mandy feeding the birds by hand without suffering a single peck. The birds were happily cooing and Mandy was singing softly. "It's amazing how love works, isn't it Paddy?"

"Yes it is," agreed the old bird keeper. "I told her she would love them someday; yes I did."

Chapter Eight

"Rocco," shouted Santa, "what's going on with the computers now?" Rocco appeared in Santa's doorway. "I can't get my computer to send any emails, or anything else for that matter."

"I know, Santa," answered Rocco, "everybody in the whole village is having the same problem, and I suspect it may be kingdom-wide."

"Blasted computers," mumbled Santa. "I've got to answer these letters, and there is a stack of order forms that I have to send out to our factories. Tell Mollie that I need some paper and envelopes, and get Mandy over here as soon as you can."

A few minutes after Mollie Makeshift delivered his favorite kind of paper and envelopes, Mandy knocked on Santa's door. "You wanted to see me, Santa?"

"Come in," answered the big guy as he motioned for her to take a chair. "Please sit down Mandy; I have a bit of a problem to discuss with you. The computers have gone completely crazy; I can't even send an email, and I have a lot of letters to write."

Mandy dropped her eyes and stared at the floor. "I know all about the problems I've caused with the computers, and I'm really and truly sorry for it. I've apologized to everybody, including you, Santa."

"No, no, Mandy, that's not why you're here. I know you're sorry; I forgave you and everyone else has, too. I sent for you because I need to write some letters, and in order to do that I must have some pens. I need for you to bring me the finest feathers you have. Just tell the Genpuni that you are in need of feathers for Santa's Pens and they will help you."

"I can do that," said Mandy excitedly. "I'll bring them today as soon as I can gather them. But tell me, Santa, why do you have to use the Genpuni feathers as pens? Why can't you use a regular pen like everyone else uses?"

"That's part of the magic of the Kingdom of Claus, Mandy. Any letters that I write on paper that leaves the kingdom must be written with a pen fashioned from the feather of a Genpuni, or else the ink will simply fade away to nothing and my letter would be no more than a blank page."

"Wow," said Mandy, "I didn't know that."

"There's a bit more for you to learn yet my dear," replied Santa, laughing softly. "Now, hurry back with those feathers, I'm so far behind on my letters now that it may take me until after Christmas to get them all written."

Chapter Nine

For five weeks Santa spent ten hours a day writing letters and corresponding with suppliers and such. Mandy kept him well supplied with the finest of the Genpuni feathers. Since she came by almost every day, their relationship grew stronger and stronger. Santa loved this little Elf with all of his big heart, and through her actions he was convinced that she was well on her way to being completely cured of her mischiefitus.

Since the computer systems were working no better, Santa had resolved to do everything by hand rather than fight the aggravation of a machine that would not work right. In fact, he was enjoying using the trusty Genpuni feather pens so much that his personal computer on his desk had not even been turned on in weeks. That was about to change. Suddenly, and much to Santa's surprise, his computer came on all by itself, and he had an urgent email waiting to be read.

```
Dear Santa,
     I  am  now  in  complete  control  of  your
computer.  You  will  not  be  able  to  send  any
emails  except  to  me  from  now  on.  Soon  all  the
computers  in  the  Kingdom  of  Claus  will  be
under  my  control  because  you  will  no  longer
be  able  to  repair  all  the  damages  I  have
done.  The  computers  that  will  work  will  only
do  what  I  tell  them  to  do,  when  I  tell  them.
That  silly  little  Elf,  Mandy  Mayflower,  did  an
excellent  job  installing  all  sorts  of  viruses
and  crazy-acting  programs  on  your  computer
systems.  LOL.  Christmas  is  not  going  to  be
```

the same without you, fat guy! Get used to it,
Santa, there's a new boss in town.

Your friend, Elf Evil Elderberry, Emperor of
Elderberryland

P.S. Ho Ho Ho.

Although surprised, Santa was not totally surprised. Deep down inside he knew that Evail Elderberry had to be behind all of this. Yet there was no time to dwell on Evail right now; he must let Rocco know about this immediately so they can finalize their plans to stop this madness before it gets any worse. The Christmas season was only a short time away, and it would *never* do for Christmas to be disrupted!

Part Three
Sneaky Santa and Mischievous Mandy

Chapter Ten

Rocco was horrified at the email that Santa had read out loud to him. Somehow Santa had managed to print the nasty note before his computer shut down again. Poor Rocco's eyes bulged and his mouth hung open in utter disbelief at this disturbing bit of news.

"How in the world can anyone be so mean, Santa? How could he be so evil? What are we going to do? Do you really think the plan we talked about will work? Good grief, Santa, I'm *really* worried. We may not be able to have Christmas anymore."

"Oh, Rocco," replied Santa, "I'm a little worried, too, but not about whether there will be Christmas or not. We will *always* have Christmas! That is the gift that has been given to us all by God, our Creator, through the birth of His Son, the Baby Jesus. That will never be taken away from us. Especially by an Elf who thinks that he can change Christmas into something it's not; into something evil. Granted, we are going to have to do some things a little differently than we're used to; the way we did them in days gone by, but Rocco my friend, there *will* be Christmas, and there *will* be gifts under the trees, and in the stockings. Now send for all the Elf supervisors and we will develop a plan to make sure there will be enough toys for all the girls and boys. Then you and I will finalize our plans to foil Evail Elderberry's plans."

As soon as Rocco had left his office, Santa sent for Cassie Carvanna. He had a plan to lift the spirits of all the hard-working Elves.

Cassie was known throughout the kingdom as the ultimate party planner. In fact, that was her title: Cassie Carvanna, Ultimate Party Planner for the

Kingdom of Claus.

"Cassie, you must keep this to yourself and your staff until I make the announcement at the noon hour. We are going to have a celebration this evening at eight o'clock for everyone in the kingdom." Santa laughed out loud at the look of surprise on Cassie's face. "Don't look so surprised," he laughed. "You should be used to my spur-of-the-moment plans after all these decades. We will hold the event in the Great Hall of Trees. Now before you say anything, I know we usually only hold Christmas Celebrations there, but this is a special occasion in our history."

"But Santa," Cassie sputtered. "For everybody, and on such short notice? I'll have to call in my entire staff to make this happen." Then she cringed. "And the Hobart's are on vacation in Greenland exploring glacier caves. Hinny Hobart is my chief baker, you know, and her husband Hank is over all the setup and decorations people. I really don't know if I could pull this off even if they were here."

Santa shrugged his shoulders. "Call them back, call the Hobart's back. They can be back just after sunset and in ample time to help you get everything ready. Let them resume their vacation tomorrow evening; give them an extra week off for their troubles. And call the Elf supervisors if you think you might need more help. The factories and shops are all shut down now anyway." Santa's cheerfulness subsided as he solemnly added, "this is extremely important, Cassie. As we speak, Rocco is gathering all the supervisors for a meeting at eleven o'clock to work out a plan for making sure we have enough toys for the very near Christmas season. This is as dark a time as I've ever seen, my friend, and we must pull together if good is to come out victorious."

"You can count on me, boss," Cassie leapt to her feet. "We will be ready at eight o'clock. The Great Hall of Trees will be decorated like you've never seen. There will be every kind of cookie, cake, and candy imaginable. There will be hot chocolate and cold milk, and water for those who want neither of them. I will display my finest gingerbread houses and hang ice bubbles everywhere. The spirits of everyone in the kingdom will be lifted."

"I knew I could count on you, Cassie. I have always been able to count on you." Santa threw back his head with a hearty laugh. "So be off with you, my trusty Elf, so I can work on these other plans."

Chapter Eleven

"We'll have to break out some of the tools and design plans that have been in storage for way too many years," declared Santa to the gathering of Elf supervisors. "We have become far too dependent on computers to do our thinking for us, as well as a lot of the actual work that we used to do." Santa couldn't help but notice frowns on the faces of a number of the supervisors. "Now, I'm not here to speak evil of the computer systems, although they wouldn't realize it even if I did. After all they are only machines and really our troubles are not their fault. They're only as smart and as good as the information we or, in this case, someone else puts into them."

A few, "Here, Here's," went up from some of the more mature Elves that probably had similar feelings toward computers as the big boss did.

"However," Santa raised his voice just enough to ensure everyone's attention, "it is time that we show the computers who's really in charge." More cheers went up. "I have written several hundred letters to hopeful children along with dozens of inquiries to our outside suppliers over the past few weeks. Not on my computer, mind you, and then printed out on paper by another machine. No, each one was written by hand with a pen fashioned from the feathers of the trusty Genpuni."

Santa looked into the eyes of the fifty or so Elves that were quietly glaring at him. "I know what you're thinking, my friends. I, too, have become much too dependent on machines to do my work. First there were typewriters, then word processors, then computers, and then even more powerful computers. But still these machines do only what we tell them to do. This is true with all the machines and tools in the kingdom: the saws, hammers, drills, presses, and all tools that have been idle for so long. So, let us take up all the tools and skills that we possess and make this a memorable Christmas season. Let goodness overcome the evil that threatens us and the entire world."

The Elf supervisors cheered and clapped their hands together. Santa had convinced them that they could indeed find a way to overcome the problems of the kingdom. "One more thing, supervisors, and this needs to stay in this room. We know where this evil threat comes from, and Rocco and I are about to finalize our plan to put an end to this nonsense. We are going to give the culprit a dose of his own medicine." More cheers were heard, and soon plans were coming together to ensure that there would be enough toys for the quickly approaching Christmas. Confident that things were in good hands and on track, Santa excused himself from the meeting, but not before informing the supervisors of the celebration at the Great Hall of Trees. Half an hour later everyone in the entire kingdom knew about the planned celebration, and were excitedly talking about it among themselves.

Chapter Twelve

Later that same afternoon Rocco reported to Santa's office. "The computer guys have finished their projects, Santa. They have installed all the programs on these flash drives, just like you instructed." Rocco handed Santa a small box containing several flash drives.

"Has everything been tested?" asked the big guy.

"Oh yes sir," replied Rocco. "They plugged them into some computers that were not part of the system and therefore not affected by Mandy Mayflower's handiwork." Rocco chuckled for an instant before catching Santa's frown. "Sorry Santa, I couldn't resist that."

"Well, did they work as planned?" asked Santa.

"Oh yeah....they're amazing, Santa." Rocco chuckled once more. "The happiest, most musical computers in the whole world. All of the positive messages and your greetings work perfectly. But I'm still not quite clear about how you intend to deliver them to Evail Elderberry, and even if you get them into his hands, why would he just plug them into his computers?"

"He wouldn't, Rocco, that's for sure," replied Santa with a broad smile on his face. "But I don't think he will have a clue as to how we could use his own devious plan against him, on his own computers.

"Yeah, Santa, I agree, but I still don't understand how we'll get those things plugged into his computers."

Before Santa could elaborate there was a soft knock on his office door.

"With a spy, Rocco, just like Evail did to us. Come on in Mandy. I've been expecting you."

Elf Mandy Mayflower entered Santa's office with a fresh supply of Genpuni feathers. "Oh, I'm sorry," she exclaimed, "I didn't mean to interrupt your meeting." Mandy's face reddened as she humbly cast her eyes to the floor. "I'll just leave the feathers here on the table, and then I'll be on my way." She quickly placed the bundle of feathers on the table and started for the door.

"Wait, Mandy, wait!" Santa hastily exclaimed. "Don't go yet; I need to discuss something with you."

"Sure, Santa," immediately Mandy's mind began to race; she wondered if she had done something else out of order. The little Elf's eyes were wide with anticipation, and Santa clearly saw through her uneasiness, just as he always did.

"Have a seat, Mandy." Santa softened his voice in an attempt to make Mandy feel more comfortable; still she sat only on the very edge of the chair she chose.

"Mandy," Santa began, his words spoken as compassionately as he could possibly manage. "We need to talk about your mischiefitus." Santa's heart ached for the little Elf as she turned red again and dropped her head. "Mandy, I'm sure your mother has told you that the memory of your condition will fade away once you are completely cured. The memory of all the mischievous things you did will also fade away; you will have no memory of the trouble you've caused and therefore you will suffer no more guilt. Guilt is the third part of your condition, you know: happiness and bliss, then anger, and now guilt."

Tears trickled down Mandy's cheeks. "I know, Santa," she nodded her head, "I want to forget but I can't. I remember every detail of everything I did like it was yesterday, and it *does* make me feel guilty. Mother says that I must be patient, but it's hard; sometimes I even have bad dreams about all the bad things I did."

Santa moved from behind his big desk and knelt in front of the sad and sobbing young Elf. He gently took her in his arms for a big hug and patted her on the back. "Now, now my sweet Mandy, everything will be all right. Soon all of this will be behind you." Santa continued to pat her on the back as she tried to stop her tears. "In the meantime, my trusty little Elf, Rocco and I would like to talk to you about putting what's left of your mischiefitus to good use."

Rocco's mouth dropped open as he suddenly realized just what this plan involved. Could Santa Claus possibly be considering sending Mandy Mayflower to the South Pole, he thought.

At the same time Mandy's head jerked from Santa's big shoulder; her eyes wide open with curiosity. "Will it help me get over all this," she asked excitedly, "I'll do almost anything to get over this mischiefitus."

"I'm not sure that it will, Mandy, but it will sure help us save Christmas as we know it." Santa watched as the twinkle in Mandy's eyes faded with his words of doubt.

After a few seconds she nodded and indicated that she was still willing to help. "What do you want me to do, Santa?"

"Mandy, you remember plugging all those flash drives into our computers, right? Well that's when most of our problems started. To undo the damages that we've suffered and to try to insure that it never happens again, our computer guys have designed a set of programs to do it for us. The hard part will be plugging our flash drives into the computers that are now controlling ours."

"That's real easy, Santa," Mandy said matter of factually and shrugged her shoulders. "All you have to do is plug them in."

"Well, Mandy," said the big guy, blowing out a slow breath, "it's not quite that simple. The computers that we need to plug our flash drives into are at the South Pole."

"The South Pole!" squealed Mandy. "*Seriously?*"

"Seriously," assured Santa. He then went on to tell her the story of Evail Elderberry and the chaos he'd caused over a number of Christmas seasons. Then Santa told her of how he had expelled Evail from the Kingdom of Claus to live out his days at the South Pole. Mandy shuttered at the thought of being cast out of the kingdom.

Santa was a little concerned that the story might distress the young Elf into thinking that the same thing could have happened to her, but instead her concern was for him. "Oh, Santa," she said, "how hard it must have been for you to send Evail away. You love everybody so much; it must have broken your heart."

"Indeed it did break my heart," a tear escaped Santa's eye and quickly disappeared into his silvery-white beard, "and for that reason I will never give up the hope that lives in my heart that someday Evail Elderberry will forsake his evil ways."

"I will help you hope, Santa." Mandy threw her arms around Santa's neck and squeezed him hard. "I will help you hope in my heart, and do anything else I can to help. I know that I can get those things plugged into Evail's computers, but Santa, how do I get to the South Pole; it's a far-away place isn't it?"

"Thank you, Mandy, I knew I could count on you. Getting you to the South Pole will be the easy part. What you have to do once you're there is the tough part. When I sent Evail and his followers down there they went on the Harsh North Wind, which is the harshest of all winds that blow. They blow only once a year, on the day after Christmas."

"Well," puffed Mandy, "I guess that explains why that Elf Tripper just showed up here the day after Christmas. To think, I thought he was my friend!"

"Yes," said Santa, "and I strongly suspect that he's well hidden somewhere in the kingdom until he can catch the Harsh North Wind back to the South Pole on the day after Christmas. Evail and the others do not know of the other way to go back and forth."

"The other way?" questioned Mandy.

"On the Sun's Twinkle," Santa answered. "As you look to the west just as the sun is setting, it's that last twinkle you see before the sun slips below the horizon. That twinkle holds a portion of the magic of the Kingdom of Claus and can take you anywhere in the world. It's a very nice ride, too, not at all like the Harsh North Wind which is very cold and bumpy."

"Okay, when do I leave?" Mandy stood, smoothed her clothes and stated that she was ready.

Santa chuckled and urged her to sit back down. "Not today; here's the plan, Mandy. Since Elf Tripper is the only one who would know who you are, you must go before he gets back to the South Pole. You will be somewhat safe before he gets back. Between now and when you leave we will work on things you must remember to say to avoid trouble. I know this is not what you want to do, but let that little bit of mischief that is still inside of you be your guide and sneak into Evail's place and plug those flash drives into his computers."

Mandy glared at the big boss. "That's sneaky Santa. We make a good team; Sneaky Santa and Mischievous Mandy." They all shared a laugh before continuing with their plans.

The busy day concluded with one of the biggest celebrations the Kingdom of Claus had ever seen. Cassie Carvanna had surely outdone herself with her preparations. Every Elf in the kingdom was there, and they all danced, sang, and dined. In spite of all the trouble they were enduring, Santa was certain that this was the happiest he had ever seen the Elves.

Chapter Thirteen

A few short weeks later all plans were in place and Mandy was prepared to make the journey of a lifetime. Santa Claus had helped her make a list of things she would need and she once again carefully checked to make sure she had all those items in a canvas bag. "A heavy cloak," she said aloud, "scarf, mittens, ear muffs, extra warm socks, my toothbrush, and this warm blanket." She closed the bag and securely tied the draw cord. "I have everything, Mother, so I guess I'm ready to go."

"Yes dear," said Mrs. Mayflower, "I'm sure you do. You have checked your bag three times today." Mother Mayflower gazed at her daughter who did not answer her next question. "Are you afraid, Mandy?" Mandy simply looked at her mother, her expression pleading for understanding that this was something she had to do. "Well," Mother Mayflower stated with a shaky voice and through tears that trickled down her rosy, plump cheeks, "I'm afraid for you."

Elves are by nature very happy creatures. Their faith in God is so deep and strong in their hearts that they hardly ever worry about anything. Sadness and fear and worry; emotions that are as rare as tears from their eyes, are experienced by only a few, at this moment, however, Mother Mayflower felt an abundance of all three.

Mandy rushed into her mother's arms. "I'll be alright, Mother, you don't have to worry about me. Please don't cry. Santa's plan is a good plan, Mother, and he promised me that if I'm not back by Christmas Eve's Eve he will come for me himself."

Mother Mayflower, in spite of trusting Santa's plan, couldn't help herself; she would worry about her daughter. She'd had two daughters, then four sons before the girl in her arms had come along, her third daughter. The daughter destined to be plagued with mischiefitus, but still her baby and she *would* worry about her.

Mandy pulled free at the sound of the knock on the door. "That will be Santa, Mother, it's time for us to go."

A hour later Santa and Mandy reached a clearing near the top of Mount Christmas. Mandy had often admired the beauty of this place from afar but this was her first visit to the mystical mountain. Santa had explained that it is best to start ones journey from a high place. They hopped down from the sleigh into knee-deep snow and as the young Elf looked around, she could see that they were indeed at the highest place in the kingdom.

"We'll have to walk the rest of the way," Santa shouted above the howling wind. "We have to go up there." He pointed to a rocky outcropping a few hundred feet up a narrow and winding trail. "Watch your step, Mandy, it's a long way down."

Never had a colder or fiercer wind blown down in the lower lands of the kingdom. Mandy's long black hair whipped about her in a fury and the tiny ice particles stung her face like a thousand pricks of a pin. She held tightly to Santa's strong hand in hopes that he would keep her from being blown from the mountain. Will we ever get there, she thought, just as she came to realize that the wind was no longer blowing. Her hair hung still and her face no longer stung from the ice. Mandy looked up; they were there.

"Santa," Mandy exclaimed, "what happened to the wind? And it's warm here. I don't understand this place." She looked all around but all she could see was a thick fog at their feet, no trail, no low lands below, nothing but fog.....and a crystal clear sky above. Mandy looked at Santa Claus with wonder.

"The wind," he laughed, "is down there." He pointed in the direction from which they came. "And you will never understand this place, for this place is not meant to be understood." Santa took Mandy's little shoulders in his hands and turned her toward the setting sun. "Be brave, my little friend. Be safe and, just like the Genpuni that you have come to love, come home to the place where you belong."

With Santa's next words the last ray of the setting sun struck Mandy in a golden glow. She watched in awe as the sun twinkled before slipping below the horizon. Suddenly she felt so sleepy she could no longer keep her eyes open.

"Watch where you're going, you clumsy girl!" The man's voice was as loud and certainly more gruff than she'd ever heard in her whole life. A hand grabbed her by the arm and snatched her to her feet. "What do you mean running out in front of me like that? Be on your way!" The grumpy old man shoved her almost causing her to fall into the snow again. "And watch where you're going or next time you might get stepped on out here in the dark."

The old man stomped of into the darkness, leaving the poor little Elf girl shaken and disoriented. She quickly looked around at her surroundings; at least the surroundings she could see. She assumed that this was a village of some sort; there were dimly lit cottages, and apparently she was in the street, but there were no streetlights. Mandy shook her head to clear the cobwebs and patted her cheeks with her cold hands. This must be the place, she thought. It's kind of like Santa described it: dark, gloomy, *and* unfriendly. Taking one step, she almost tripped over something. "My bag," she whispered. "Now I've got to find a place to stay out of the cold." Mandy picked up her bag and turned around once more in search of shelter.

Suddenly she felt very cold......and *very* alone.

Part Four
Mandy and Marko

Chapter Fourteen

Mandy's first night at the South Pole was miserable beyond anything she could imagine. For the first time in her life, she was actually scared. She'd spent the night underneath the canvas cover of a small sleigh; a sleigh like she'd never seen before, just barely big enough for her to get into. The odor under the canvas was almost more than she could bear. It smelled like dead fish, but there was no other choice at hand. Sometime during the night she was rudely awakened by a group of men quarreling in the street from where she had just come. Peeking from her hiding place, she witnessed behaviors that were totally foreign to her. Several men were striking each other with their fists and yelling so loudly that lights began to come on in the cottages. They were stumbling around as if they couldn't properly stand upright. What in the world could be wrong with them, she thought. Wisely she resisted the urge to leave her hiding place and ask if she could help because of her fresh memory of the way the first man she'd met acted toward her. Thankfully the group soon disbanded amid the shouts and threats from the occupants of the dwellings.

Just as sleep had overtaken Mandy's tired body once again, she was awakened by the barking and howling and ferocious growling of a hundred dogs. She had never seen a dog before, except in school books, but she knew these were the sounds they made. The sun was just coming up, so she quickly exited the sleigh. She surely didn't want to get caught here. Within minutes a man appeared from around the corner of a barn-like building leading seven big, furry dogs, all of them barking and jumping at the same time. Somehow he managed to get the dogs fastened to the little sleigh, hopped onto the back, and away they went. This was without a doubt the strangest thing Mandy had ever seen! Who'd ever heard of dogs pulling a sleigh? That's what reindeer are for!

"Wow," she said softly, "things are different down here." From her hiding place between two large, wooden barrels she could still hear the yelping and barking of dogs from every direction. Every now and then she was able to catch a glimpse of one of the odd-looking sleighs as they zipped past. It seemed as though everyone and everything was in a hurry. The dogs always ran, and the people who appeared in the streets were always in a rush going to and fro. After a few hours in her hiding place, Mandy began to realize just how unhappy these people of the South Pole were. Their main means of communication seemed to be yelling and shouting at each other. It was obvious that if there had ever been love in this place, it was now as frozen as the ground she sat on. "What a shame," she whispered as she watched a man, well into his mature years, viciously reprimand a little boy for simply running by him too closely. This was very much the same treatment she'd received the evening before and her heart ached for the child.

"What's a shame?" The voice came from above her and caught her by such surprise that she squealed from fright.

Mandy slowly looked up to find that her hiding place was directly below a window, and from that window a young man leaned out and looked directly into the frightened eyes that met his.

"Who are you?" he asked, "and what are you doing here?"

Mandy shuttered, trying to remember what she was supposed to say if she were caught. I didn't waste any time getting caught, she thought, and took a deep breath; here goes. "My name is Mandy," she said boldly, "and who are you?"

"You didn't answer my second question, *Mandy. What* are you doing here?"

At least he's not yelling at me, Mandy thought, and there may even be a bit of kindness in his voice. He certainly doesn't look mean. "I'm trying to stay warm; it's cold out here you know." She hoped that her answer would prevent further questions.

"Then why don't you go home?" the boy replied.

Mandy almost shed a tear at his suggestion, but instead she just gave him a pout with her saddest expression and allowed her lower lip to protrude a bit.

"Whatever," he said, "but if you're not going home I would find another place to try and stay warm if I were you. Those are the fish-head barrels; you're probably going to get splattered." At that moment the young man reached out with a long hook and lifted the top from one of the containers. The stench struck Mandy's nose like a frozen snowball, and just as she scrambled clear of the barrels the boy tipped out a large bucket of fish-heads. He chuckled, and then replaced the lid.

Mandy looked up at the smiling young man, feeling her face redden with a combination of embarrassment and anger. "You're right. I would have been splattered," said Mandy trying to regain her composure. "What is this place anyway?"

"It's the fish house," he answered, giving her a sideways look. "Everybody knows this is the fish house. Uh, why don't you come around to the back door and warm yourself by the fire. You'll be safe here; the boss isn't working today. I think he was out too late last night....again."

"I don't know about that," Mandy was saying as the boy disappeared back inside and the window closed. "I really don't....know....you.....," her words trailed off leaving her standing alone in the narrow space between two buildings.

"Come on; it is cold out here," the words came from the back of the structure. She turned to see the boy peering around the corner.

"God, please protect me," she whispered, and started toward the boy in hopes that he might befriend her as she had befriended Tripper.

Mandy could feel the warmth from within the building as she neared the doorway, and with the warmth came smells of fresh bread and barleylew. This triggered an involuntary growl from her tummy. She turned to the young man, big eyed from embarrassment, and shrugged her shoulders. He just smiled and held the door for her. Once inside she realized that she was in the kitchen of what appeared to be living quarters.

Barleylew is her favorite breakfast food in the whole world: a cinnamon and brown sugar spiced blend of puffed barley and cream. And there it was, still warm on the stove. Her tummy growled again. How long has it been since I ate anything, she wondered; I feel really hungry. I can't remember a thing about my journey here. It may have taken days. Suddenly a memory did come to her; Santa's declaration, just before she drifted off to sleep on Mount Christmas, that she be exiled from the Kingdom of Claus until she became truly ready to return. Mandy took a deep breath knowing that was the only way that she could explain why she was here. She had been banished from the kingdom and she could truthfully make that claim.

"Are you hungry?" the boy's question brought Mandy's attention back to the present. "How long has it been since you've eaten?"

"I really don't know," stammered the girl.

"Well we can fix that," the young man said cheerfully. "Have a seat, and I will make you some breakfast. Hot sweet-water?" he asked.

Sweet-water was not her favorite but right now it sounded delicious. Mandy nodded shyly and considered his kindness. This Elf was not at all like the others she had seen down here. Maybe they weren't all bad. At least she hoped so.

Soon she was enjoying hot buttered bread and a big bowl of barleylew.

"Say, uh, Mandy, you're not from around here, are you?"

"Not really," she surely didn't want to talk about that just yet.

"Well, where are your parents?" The young man continued with his questions. "Have they been banned from the empire?"

"Not really," she repeated. "Does someone live here?" She hoped her inquiry might change the subject.

The young man frowned at Mandy's short answer, but then confidently stated that this is where he lives. "I moved here after my parents were banned from the empire. My father was the supervisor over the fish house and Vernon was the assistant who lived here. Now Vernon's the supervisor and I'm the assistant. Except that Vernon is never here, at least not to do any work. He comes by every couple of days to yell at me and threaten to have me banned from the empire if I don't keep up with production."

"Why were your parents banned from the empire?" Mandy intended to take advantage of the young man's willingness to talk. "And, by the way, what is your name?"

"Oh, sorry," he said, "my name is Marko, Marko Elderberry."

It was all Mandy could do to hold on to her spoon. She had never, ever in her entire life heard of an Elf whose first *and* last name didn't start with the same letter, but now she was talking to one who says his name is Marko *Elderberry*. That's even stranger than those noisy dogs pulling sleighs.

To Mandy's relief Marko continued his story without showing that he'd detected her surprise. "Yeah, both my father and mother were banned from the empire for being part of a group that was trying to overthrow the Emperor. They have been gone for more than a year now, living just outside the boundary of the empire. I am allowed to see them from a distance, but I can't talk to them. My two older brothers and my three sisters are there also. I probably would have been gone, too, except for my age; they said I was too young to know what was going on, although I did know." Marko shrugged his shoulders. "Or maybe they just needed someone who knew how to run the fish house."

"That's terrible," shrieked Mandy. "Where do they live; what do they eat?"

"Ice caves, they live in ice caves," Marko's voice was sad sounding, "and all they have to eat is fish. They are made to fish all the time and almost all of their catch is brought here for the empire. The banned people are allowed to keep just enough for themselves to keep from starving."

"Marko, that's the most horrible thing I've ever heard of," shrieked Mandy again as she jumped to her feet.

Marko smiled; he sensed a rare honesty in his visitor. "You're really not from around here are you? I can't believe you don't know about all this: the raids in people's homes at night, and banning folks even with no evidence against them. There are more than a hundred people out there on the ice plains, just barely surviving."

Mandy shrugged her shoulders. "Why did your parents want to overthrow the Emperor? Is he that bad?"

"Bad!" shouted Marko, "you really don't know! He's the worst a Sleve can be!" Marko stood shaking his head. "You must have lived your entire life under an iceberg. I can't believe you could be so....so....innocent." He started for the door on the opposite side of the room. "I have to go back to work now, but if you'd like to come back around at suppertime, you're welcome to."

Mandy watched as he left the kitchen through a hallway leading to the fish house. He's cute, she thought, really cute when he's a little riled up. I may have found a friend to help me with my task here. He's obviously not a friend of the Emperor, Evail Elderberry. Mandy was deep in thought concerning her mission, and sipping what was left of her hot sweet-water, when Marko reappeared in the doorway. He stepped forward and placed a book on the table in front of her.

"I suppose you've never heard of this guy either," he said dryly, "but I thought you might like something to read." Then he left again.

Mandy reached for the book; her heart skipped a beat as she recognized the figure on the faded and battered cover. "Santa Claus," she whispered. "He knows who you are." She opened the old book and began to read, "The Story of Santa and the Kingdom of Claus," as she'd read a dozen times before.

Later that morning Mandy discovered that several pages had been removed from the book. "Oh that's terrible," she whispered to herself, "some of the best and most important parts are missing." Right then she decided that she would have to broach the subject of Santa Claus very carefully and, at the same time, play dumb and see just what and how much this young man knew about the jolly, round fellow in the book, the North Pole, and the subject of Christmas.

Chapter Fifteen

Marko half expected to find Mandy still in the kitchen when he finished his work for the day. He was a little sad that she wasn't, but the kitchen was cleaned spotlessly and there was a note on the table. He smiled as he read the simple message of thanks and the promise that she'd be back at suppertime. Immediately he went to work on the evening meal preparations. Suddenly there was a sharp rap at his door. Throwing the door open he expected to see Mandy's pretty face, but surprisingly he found himself gazing at a scowling face belonging to a guard from the Empire Employment System.

"Marko Elderberry?" the guard grunted.

Marko nodded yes and asked how he could be of service.

"You know this girl?" He jerked Mandy from behind him. "She claims that she's your friend and that you are expecting her. Is there any truth to that?"

"Why, yes sir," Marko was used to having to quickly compose himself for the guards and other empire officials. "She is my friend, and I was expecting her back by suppertime."

The guard rubbed his chin and studied Marko. "Where does she live?" The guard set his jaw thinking that he'd tricked the boy with an unexpected question. "No one seems to know her," he added.

"She lives here," Marko answered calmly. "And the reason why hardly anybody knows her is that she's so bashful and backwards and completely without social skills. You remember that Sleve, Lucas Elderberry and his wife that were banned, don't you?" Marko did not give the guard time to answer. "And you also remember that they had twelve or thirteen daughters." The guard nodded. "Well, most of the girls were adopted into other families but some of the older ones had to make it on their own. I'm just trying to help the poor Sleve out to keep her from starving."

"Well, keep an eye on her," the guard finally mumbled, shoving her toward the doorway. "She was snooping around like she was up to something."

"I will, sir, thank you," replied Marko as he stepped aside to allow Mandy to enter. Mandy turned to the guard and gave him a childish wave, in hopes of shoring up Marko's story. But in her head the words bashful, backwards, and without social skills were ringing like Christmas bells.

"That was a close one," muttered Marko, "those guards give me the creeps." Then he returned to his supper preparations. "I hope you like fish," he added, but his inquiry went unanswered. Finally he turned to his guest who was glaring coldly at him. "What?" he asked.

"Bashful, backwards, and completely without social skills?" Mandy's face was red and her black eyes told of her displeasure. "I'll have you know that I am *not* bashful, or backwards, and I probably have more social skills than you.... why you're not even truthful....you fibbed to that guard. I don't live here!"

"Sure you do, right out there in the tool shed," he pointed out the window to a small shed in the back yard. "I've already figured out that you don't have a place to call home. The shed is dry and well insulated so you'll be warm and comfortable there, and don't worry I have plenty of blankets and pillows."

Considering her new-found friend's generous, and risky proposal, Mandy's anger level subsided just a bit. "You still fibbed, though. I'm not one of Lucas Elderberry's daughters."

"I never said that you were," stated Marko. "That guard just assumed that you were. You're lucky that he did, or else you could be on your way to the ice plains now."

"Well," sighed Mandy, "it was still sneaky."

Marko nodded and mumbled, "you should know about sneaky," then returned to his supper preparations.

With the evening meal before them, they ate slowly and shared small talk. Eventually Marko began to tell about his family.

"My great-grandfather, we call him GG, came here with the Emperor many, many decades ago. They were friends in the old country, and great-grandfather said the Emperor could talk just about anybody into anything. He talked a lot of people into settling this new land with him, and by the time everyone realized it was a mistake it was too late. All talk and remembrance of the old country was prohibited and soon most people just forgot. Mostly, everybody was concentrating on survival. I remember GG's stories of how he had been deceived by his friend and how hard it was when they first came here. Everyone was unhappy and despised this place; they all wanted to go back to the old country, but the Emperor wouldn't allow it. Sleves were assigned jobs and told what to do; they were watched every minute of the day and night."

"What's a Sleve?" interrupted Mandy, "I've heard you say that word before."

Marko shook his head in wonder at the young lady seated at his table. "Mandy, we're Sleves. Where *are* you from?"

"We'll talk about that later. Go on with your story."

Marko hesitated, glaring at his new friend, but then continued. "GG used to tell us wonderful stories of a distant land called the North Pole where everyone lived in peace and harmony. People worked at factories where toys were made and at shops where cookies and candies and cakes were made. A special time of year, called Christmas, was celebrated by unconditional giving. That means giving something to someone without expecting anything in return."

Mandy impatiently nodded that she understood.

"Did you look at the book I gave you earlier?"

"I did," exclaimed Mandy, "I read every word of it. Tell me, Marko, what do you know about this Santa Claus? He sounds like a nice man."

Marko smiled warmly. "According to GG he's the best. Santa Claus would deliver toys all over the world on Christmas Eve. Christmas is the birthday of the Baby Jesus, but I don't know much about Him. We are forbidden to talk about Santa Claus or Jesus. Get caught talking about them and that's an instant ticket to the ice plains. I guess that's why my grandfather never shared those stories with us. My father, however, memorized them all thanks to GG and loved sharing them with my brothers and sisters and me." Marko stopped speaking, took a deep breath and shrugged his shoulders. "A lot of Sleves don't believe any of the old stories. They say that Jesus and Santa Claus doesn't exist, and that they are just tales that somebody made up as entertainment.

They also say that Christmas is just a fairy tale and giving gifts to each other is a crazy myth. Our lives are not at all like that, Mandy. The Emperor says that we Sleves are here to serve him and the empire; our welfare is of no concern, and we shouldn't be concerned about each other. But, Mandy, I feel in my heart that there is another way of life. My great-grandfather knew that way of life. I know he's not nuts like all the keepers say, even if he is in the......, you know, he's being taken care of in that place where really old people go."

Mandy had to concentrate very hard to keep from looking shocked at everything Marko told her, but still she wanted to hear more. "Then you really believe in Christmas and all that stuff in that book you gave me?"

"I do!" Mandy was a little surprised by his plain and definite answer. "I believe that Jesus and Christmas and Santa Claus are real."

"How about the other Elves, do others believe like you do?"

"*Elves?*" Marko cocked his head sideways as Mandy flushed a slight red. "What are you talking about?"

"I mean Sleves," she quickly corrected herself.

"Sure they do," replied the young man, "but those of us who do are very careful who we talk to. I mean, I don't really know you, and I could be talking to a spy for the Emperor right now. I might even be on my way to the ice plains tomorrow.

Mandy chuckled and squeezed Marko's hand. "If I am a spy, I'm certainly not a spy for the Emperor. Thank you for supper, Marko. I'll clean up the kitchen."

"While you do that I'll get you some blankets, a pillow, and a candle. First, though, will you please tell me one thing about yourself. I've told you so much, and the only thing I know about you is your name."

"Sure," she sang out and opened her canvas bag to retrieve the book he'd given her that morning. Handing it back to him, her eyes twinkled like little stars in the sky. "I will tell you that I already have a copy of this book at home. I have read it many, many times, and today I read it again."

"*Home!*" Marko jumped to his feet. "You said home. Where *is* your home?"

Mandy smiled. "You said one thing."

Chapter Sixteen

For eight days Mandy lived a very secretive life. While Marko worked during the daytime she would make quick trips through the village learning the locations of all the buildings that were important to the empire. On two separate occasions she was sure that she'd seen the Emperor himself; a very old and stooped man wearing a spotted fur cloak and an awkward looking crown of sorts on his hairless head.

"Yeah, that's him alright," Marko told her when she described the old man she'd seen in the fancy large sleigh with the double team of dogs. "He's as old as GG, and I think he'll live forever."

During these days, Marko and Mandy shared every breakfast and evening meal together. Every day Mandy would share a single bit of information about herself with her new friend, and this day was no different as Marko sat waiting anxiously at the table as she cleared the dishes.

"My last name is Mayflower," she said.

Marko laughed. "Don't be silly, your name is Elderberry just like everybody else." He made a waving motion with his hands suggesting that she give him something. "Now come on; I'm being patient."

"It most certainly *is not* Elderberry," she insisted. "My name is Mayflower!" The girl's eyes blazed again like the time when he had accused her of having no social skills.

Marko leaned back in his chair and folded his arms across his chest and studied Mandy's face. How could that be, he thought. Everybody was named Elderberry; that was the law of the empire. *Everybody* is an Elderberry, and if you have the same first name as someone else your number was used to tell you apart. Everybody has a number, too. "What's your number?" he blurted out, trying to catch her off guard.

"What?" she replied.

"Everybody has a number; what's your number?"

"I don't have a number, Marko!" Now she was getting a little irritated. "And why would you think my name is Elderberry? You don't know my family."

"*Everybody* is named Elderberry;" he protested as firmly as he could manage. "That's the law."

"Are you serious?" Mandy shook her head in wonder; the more she learned about this place the weirder it became. Maybe it's time to go out on a limb, she thought. I pray that he is a true friend.

"Marko," she began, "are you truly my friend? Can I completely trust you, even with my very existence?"

Without speaking, Marko reached out over the table and Mandy did the same; with a firm handshake they sealed their friendship and trust in one another.

Mandy took a deep breath and let it out with a sigh. "Marko," she began, "what I'm about to tell you could be the end of me if the wrong people find out." Marko made a crossing sign over his heart and then zipped his lips. "I am not a Sleve, Marko. I am an Elf, and I'm here from the North Pole. Santa Claus sent me here on a mission."

For the next hour Mandy told her trusty new friend everything she knew about Christmas, the Baby Jesus, Santa Claus, and Evail Elderberry.

Marko was stunned, but still he believed every word he heard from Mandy.

"If any of this falls into the wrong hands it will be the end of both of us, Mandy Mayflower. I promise that I will do everything I can to help you." Marko shook his head from side to side. "Wow, I can't believe you actually know Santa Claus.

Part Five
Mission Accomplished

Chapter Seventeen

By the end of her third week in this foreign and inhospitable land, Mandy and Marko were well on their way to having a plan in place…a plan that would not only free the computers in the Kingdom of Claus from the control of the evil Emperor, but free the people from his rule as well, at least those who wanted to be freed.

"Okay, Mandy," said Marko, "I have some valuable information. I got it from GG when I went to visit him yesterday evening. He told me that in six days, during the Emperor's Summer Moon, there will be a big celebration at the ice palace with lots of food and strong drink and three days of Penguin flogging. All the top officials of the empire will be there at the same time."

"Wait, Marko," Mandy's voice sounded stressed. "Did you tell GG of our plans?" She had met GG on two occasions and, although she thought him a lovely man and loved him at once, she felt that at his mature age Marko's great-grandfather might not remember that some things are to be kept secret. Her fears were relieved, however, when Marko explained to her that he had mentioned not one whisper of their plan; GG had simply volunteered the information.

"It was like he knew we needed to know about this," insisted Marko. "GG says that this is one of two secret meetings which takes place each year. The meeting during the wintertime is for dogfights and sled races. I can see the sled races, but why would anybody want to watch dogs fighting, or those poor Penguins being flogged with a whip?"

"Hold on a minute," Mandy held up her hands in front of her face. "What do you mean summer moon, it's the middle of winter now, and what is a Penguin?"

Marko laughed. "Oh no, my friend, it's the middle of summer. If it were winter it would really be cold. A Penguin is a black and white bird that is almost as tall as we are; they have tiny wings and they can't fly at all, but they swim in water better and faster than a fish. They waddle around like this." He stood, holding his knees tightly together as he walked, or rather waddled. "They go pretty fast though. Some Sleves think it's funny to chase them around and flog them with a leather whip. Personally, I think it's cruel!"

Mandy sat quietly for a few seconds after hearing this. Her thoughts were of how differently the culture and behavior of these people had developed down here at the South Pole. She knew it was a direct result of their leadership and she felt sorry for them all. Is there any hope for these people, she asked herself, when suddenly Santa's words, 'I still have hope in my heart,' filled her head and she latched onto that same hope as tightly as she could. If Santa still had hope, so could she.

For the next few minutes she and Marko talked of happier things. She told him about the Genpuni of the North Pole and how Santa Claus uses the feathers they shed to write letters. She told him that reindeer were used to pull sleighs and how the kingdom would hold celebrations that *everyone* attends. No Elves or animals are ever mistreated, and if they ever were, the abuser would suffer the wrath of their fellow Elves.

"It's the best place in the world, Marko. Sure it's cold and the wind blows sometimes, but warm hearts make it all worth it. I wish you could see it, Marko, it's such a beautiful place. Twinkling lights are everywhere, and trees too, real live trees, like the ones in the book you lent me." Suddenly she noticed that the sparkle in Marko's eyes was gone. Reaching for his hand she made him a promise. "I can't take you back with me, although I wish I could, but once I'm back I'll talk to Santa Claus and see what can be done."

A tear trickled down Marko's face and he smiled. "Thank you, Mandy, but I can't, my family is here."

Mandy's heart ached for her friend at that very moment, and the only thing she knew to do was ask God to watch over him and all of his family.

Chapter Eighteen

"Knowing about this big celebration will make it much easier to get to the Emperor's computers," said Mandy, "but I'm still concerned about the handful of guards that will still be stationed there."

"Good fortune is with us, my friend," replied Marko, "all of the computers are in one place. The Emperor wouldn't allow anyone else to have one, so they're all right there." His head bobbed to one side drawing her attention to the structure they'd been watching for two weeks from behind sleighs, barrels, or the shadows of buildings. A guard had exited the building and pulled a small container from his pocket; looking from side to side until he was satisfied no one was watching, he took a quick drink. "That's strong drink, Mandy, it makes them act crazy, and if they have enough of it they'll fall down and go to sleep."

"Tell me once more about your plan to distract the guards. Only two more days, Marko, and things will either be very different around here or we'll be on our way to the ice plains." She smiled at her friend, but he knew she was nervous about what she had to do.

"My cousin, Matt, has a pack of dogs," he said, "the worst dogs you'll ever see. They can't get along for five minutes without having a big fight. He's going to drive his sled right up to the front of that building and let them go at it. You, my friend, will slip in when the guards come out to see what's going on. Matt is going to stumble around and pretend like he's had a tummy full of strong drink. Those guards will search him and his sled for the strong drink and, at the same time, the dogs will be causing a bunch of commotion. You should have ten, maybe fifteen minutes, to get to the computers."

Mandy smiled again. "That kind of sounds like fun," she giggled as she imagined the guard's frustration of not finding what they so wanted to find.

"Maybe so," chuckled Marko, "I just hope they don't treat my cousin too badly. They'll probably strike him with their fists and give him a few kicks.

Don't worry about him, though, Matt knows a few bruises are well worth the effort."

"And don't you worry about me either," Mandy squeezed Marko's hand. She knew she would be all right. Even if she were caught, she had the comforting thought that Santa Claus himself would come to her rescue.

Chapter Nineteen

Two days later everything was in place for the big mission. At the exact moment when Mandy and Marko were walking past the headquarters of the computer systems a sled, heavy-laden with many boxes and bundles and containing almost everything imaginable, except strong drink, pulled to a stop just feet from them. The driver of the sled cautiously tossed a handful of fish among the seven rowdy dogs, instantly inciting a violent free-for-all. Even after the fish were gone, the fight continued. Within seconds, both of the guards who were on duty that evening were outside investigating the commotion. Just as planned, when the guards saw Marko's cousin, Matt, staggering around and bellowing at his dogs, they immediately suspected him of being under the influence of strong drink. They smiled at each other, and soon had him wrestled to the ground. With snow flying in all directions, everyone yelling, and dogs fighting virtually on top of the three men, not a single person noticed Mandy slip into the building through the door from which the guards had just exited.

Finding the computers was the easiest part of her job. There they were, right in front of her, in a big room in the middle of the building. Mandy went to work as fast as she could, and in a matter of minutes she had plugged flash drives into every computer in the room. Now they were all busy downloading the information. She smiled to herself because she knew in a little while Evail Elderberry would be aware that Santa Claus had worked his magic.

The guards were still rifling through the load on the sled to the chorus of barks, growls, and howls of the dogs when she slipped out the same door she'd entered and took her place at Marko's side. She slid her arm within his and gave him a gentle tug to signal him that the mission had been a complete success. The pair nodded then walked off as if nothing was going on. Once they were out of sight of the gathering of onlookers at the computer headquarters building they shared a big smile, but they were still too nervous to speak. They made up for that once they were safely in Marko's kitchen, though, as the pair hugged and laughed and danced in circles while holding on to each others hands in anticipation of what was in store for the empire.

Suddenly, and much to the surprise of the celebrating pair, the empire's loud speakers crackled to life. Then the sound of bells reached their ears. Marko's eyes were wide with wonder as he'd never heard the sound of bells before!

"Christmas Bells!" squealed Mandy, "I didn't know that would happen. The Emperor knows now." She and Marko continued to dance in circles.

"What a beautiful sound," said Marko while trying to catch his breath, "I've never heard anything like it!"

"Just wait until you hear the music!" exclaimed Mandy.

"I've never heard music, it's against the laws of the empire," he was explaining just as the sound of a harp filled the air.

The music continued all through the night and the next day. No one slept; the streets were filled with people dancing and laughing and celebrating a feeling and a happiness they had never known before. The guards and empire officials soon gave up on their attempts to control the crowds. It was obvious that there were many more Sleves against the Emperor than there were for him.

Mandy and Marko celebrated right along with the village people. She was amazed at the difference she saw. Had the people she was watching now been locked away inside the people she saw the day before? Had something as simple as music set them free?

But it seemed as though the change would be short-lived when another sound came over the loud speakers. Almost as harsh and gruff as the growls of the dogs it struck their ears. It was Evail Elderberry.

"I can't get this blasted noise to stop!" he screamed in a revolting tone, "but I can speak over it!" Even though his words were met with boos and hisses from all around the village, he continued. "My computers have been vandalized. The guards and officials are in search of the low-down Sleves who are responsible for this. If you know anything about this and don't come forward with your information you will be considered as guilty as the criminals themselves." Once again the entire village booed and heckled the Emperor. He did not hear this, however, as he was safe within his castle-like home. "When you are found out," he bellowed even louder, "and make no mistake about it you will be caught, you will not be sent to the ice plains. You will be fed to the Orca's!"

A hushed fear rippled through the crowd and whispers of what the Emperor had said was repeated by many. Decades of cruel leadership and threats from the Emperor lived deep inside his subjects and although Evail Elderberry had been harsh and hateful he had never before threatened them with being fed to the Orca's. Mandy knew that this kind of threat could send them scurrying back into their cottages. The tired but joyous Sleves held their ground, however, then laughed at and mocked the Emperor and his ridiculous rants. Very soon dancing, and laughing, and shaking hands, and hugging, and a showing of love for one another that had not been displayed in generations resumed. Mandy celebrated right along with them as if she were one of them; she was so happy for these people that tears of joy flowed freely from her eyes. Most, if not all, who filled the street had been mistreated all their lives. Their great-grandparents, and in some cases their great-great-grandparents had chosen to come to this place with the evil Evail Elderberry when he was expelled from the North Pole. Most of them soon realized their mistake, but it was too late as the Emperor refused to allow anyone to return. Future generations would pay for their choice. Eventually Mandy found an out-of-the-way place to sit on an empty wooden crate and thought about this. She thought about the day that Santa Claus had told her that everything a person did had an effect on others. She also remembered how he'd made it a point to say that there was no way of telling how long that effect might last. "You're such a smart guy," she said softly. "Now I can see even more clearly what you meant."

"Talking to yourself?" Marko asked teasingly.

"Yeah," Mandy replied with a smile. "How long do you think the Emperor will go on with his ranting and raving before he gives up?" Before Marko could answer, the harp and bell music stopped. The crowd of Sleves fell silent at the abrupt ending of such a pleasing sound. Even the Emperor stopped yelling over the loud speakers. Sleves looked at one another wondering if their rare treat was over. Had the Emperor figured out how to stop the music? Looks of dread blanketed all the people. But within seconds of the sudden silence that captured everyone's attention, another voice boomed through the village; not the shrill and harsh screams of the Emperor, but a strong, steady voice of authority embellished with friendliness and compassion. Mandy's eyes grew large, and she grasped Marko's arm with surprise.

"Santa," said Mandy lovingly. Her grip was so firm on her friend's arm that it caused him to look down at the girl's hand.

"Greetings, my friends of the South Pole. I am known as Santa Claus, of the Kingdom of Claus, of the North Pole."

A rumble moved over the crowd like a wave on the ocean's surface. Even the guards, who had taken advantage of the quiet to bark orders and lash out at a few with their leather whips, now stood in stunned silence.

Santa continued, "I trust you all have enjoyed the musical interlude. There will be more to come, but in the meantime I would like to invite you all to join me and the rest of the world in celebrating Christmas. I am aware that some of you, or maybe none of you, have ever heard of Christmas, but it is a most precious time of year when everyone celebrates the birth of Jesus, the Son of God, who is the Creator of all things. Let me assure you that the stories you may have heard about people giving gifts to one another are true. This is the way we celebrate the greatest gift of all; when God sent his Son to live His life on earth. Your leader, Evail Elderberry, has done his best to disrupt Christmas and turn it into something it's not. He has failed, and in due time you will see firsthand proof of his failure. As for now, I wish you all a Merry Christmas."

With that the music began again; this time it was stories of the birth of Jesus set to beautiful music, and songs about all things Christmas.

"They are called Christmas Carols," Mandy said to Marko, "isn't it a beautiful sound?" Then she settled back as comfortably as she could on the wooden box and marveled at the joy she saw.

Chapter Twenty

For the next eight days the music continued day and night, as did the celebrations. Almost all of the guards had abandoned their posts. They'd traded their ridiculous-looking brown and pink uniforms they were forced to wear for regular clothes, and had joined the villagers in grand celebration. The handful of guards and empire officials who remained loyal to the Emperor were nowhere to be found. Apparently the throngs of revelers had them very concerned for their safety. Even the Emperor had finally given up on trying to shout his threats over the endless music.

Life for the Sleves of the South Pole was changing; they had tasted freedom and they liked it. In spite of Evail Elderberry's many threats of withholding food and water and firing everyone from their jobs the village economy was booming. In fact the only thing in short supply was strong drink, and collectively those who on occasions partook of the drink declared they no longer wanted or needed the evil liquid. Meetings were held in public, and subjects were discussed that once would only have been whispered about behind closed doors. Soon plans were made to elect a group of leaders to govern the empire and remove the Emperor from the palace. There was really nothing Evail Elderberry could do at this point except give up.

Every Sleve who had been banned from the empire was gathered from the ice plains and welcomed back into the village as if they were heroes. In a way they were hero's. Marko was so happy to have his family back that he was beside himself. GG was even rescued from the place where old Sleves were kept. He was happy to tell many stories of his old home and the peace and happiness that existed there. GG was astonished to learn that Mandy was in fact from the North Pole, and on a special mission for Santa Claus. They spent hours together laughing and swapping stories. He couldn't believe that old Paddy was still well enough to tend to the Genpuni.

"So, Mandy Mayflower," GG said in a very low yet serious voice, "I remember the Mayflower family. You are the third daughter of a third daughter and have the mischiefitus, I take it?"

The query caught Mandy by surprise. Since she'd been so happy for the past few days she had almost forgotten who she was! Her answer came with a stare at the floor.

The old Sleve patted her hands that rested upon her lap. With a chuckle he said, "I knew your great-grandmother, Marie; I knew her when she had the mischiefitus. I would have asked for her hand in marriage if not for that other fellow. Mack, I think it was."

Mandy's head popped up to see his smiling face. "Mack is my great-grandfather! I can't believe you know him!" They both laughed as her embarrassment over her condition evaporated.

"I know all of those old Elves," GG laughed and slapped his knee, but suddenly a quiet and distant look overtook him.

"Are you okay, GG?" asked Marko's dad.

"I'm an Elf," he said softly, "we're all Elves. I had almost forgotten that."

In spite of the ensuing laughter Mandy was suddenly overwhelmed with homesickness. She knew it was time for her to return to the place she belonged. Tomorrow she would make preparations to go home. Tomorrow she would tell Marko goodbye.

Chapter Twenty-one

"I knew you would go back some day," Marko said, his voice so soft and low that she barely heard him. He wouldn't allow himself to look her in the eyes out of fear that his heartache would show. "When?"

"Today, Marko, at sunset."

His head dropped even lower, and she saw the tear as it buried itself in the snow at his feet. Reaching for her hand, he kissed it, turned and walked into the fish house.

Marko borrowed his cousin's sled and team of unruly dogs later that day and escorted Mandy Mayflower to the highest place he knew of at the edge of the ice plains. They'd packed their supper and took their last meal together on a heavy blanket spread upon the ice. Watching the sun dip farther toward the horizon, their conversation had been a little awkward. Mandy knew that the goodbyes they'd exchanged that evening were difficult for Marko to bear. She too felt the deep aching in her heart. Her mind whirled. How could Marko and she become so much more than friends in just a few short weeks? Why was Marko still paying for the wrongs of Evail Elderberry so many decades later? Why was she now feeling the effects of those same wrongs?

She belonged at the North Pole, however, and those farewells had to be said. As she walked toward the setting sun the long, brilliant, last ray of light of the day caused such a glare that it was impossible for Marko to see her. And when the last twinkle faded as the sun slipped below the horizon, she was gone.

Marko Elderberry sank to his knees in the snow, his heart breaking.

"Oh dear," exclaimed the kind voice of a lady, "you've fallen. Please let me help you up before you catch a cold there in that snow drift." The sweet elderly Elf lady helped Mandy to her feet, dusted her off and then retrieved her bag from the drift. "Are you all right?" she asked.

"I'm fine," answered Mandy, through a yawn. "Just a little sleepy. Thank you for your help." Mandy recognized the lady as the great-great-grandmother of one of her friends, but the kindly old lady didn't know who she was helping out of the snow; she was just happy to be helping. What a contrast from her first night at the South Pole when she was face first in the snow. Mandy waved goodbye to the lady then turned toward the lane where her mother and father were waiting for her at their cottage.

Naturally, Mandy's family was elated to have her back home safe and sound. Hugs and tears of joy were plentiful within the warm confines of the Mayflower cottage. Mandy's mother almost refused to allow her to report to Santa Claus as she was supposed to do.

"He'll be asleep at this hour," she'd said. "Why don't you just wait until morning."

"He will be expecting me, Mother. Santa said for me to report to him as soon as I got back. Right after I saw my family, that is."

A short time later Mandy knocked on Santa's door. "Mission accomplished," she proudly stated when Santa opened the door, and for the next hour she excitedly told him everything that she could remember that she'd done, seen, heard, experienced, felt, and thought. "What will become of them, Santa? Right now they are not under the control of that evil Evail Elderberry, but without you they may not be able to hang on to their freedom. Santa I remember when you told me how our actions affect others and how we have no way of knowing how far into the future that effect may reach, but, Santa is it fair that all generations pay for the wrongs of their ancestors? It breaks my heart to think so."

Santa Claus gathered the little Elf into his strong arms. "It has *always* broken my heart, Mandy Mayflower, but I have another plan that I will put into motion on Christmas Eve. For now, hurry back home and be with your family; come to my office in the morning and we'll talk about my plan and you can tell me more about Marko."

Part Six
Homecoming

Chapter Twenty-two

Early the next morning Santa Claus and Mandy shared hot chocolate in his office and once again she told him about all her adventures while at the South Pole. Just before her last thoughts of the day and her simple little prayer that God watch over her friend, Marko, Mandy realized that she'd failed to tell Santa some of the most important information. Now she was bursting to tell him.

"That first day," Mandy exclaimed, "I thought I was done for. When that guard grabbed me by my arm I almost fainted. I have never been so scared, Santa. I'm just thankful that Marko turned out to be such a good friend, or else I would have been treated rudely, I'm sure."

"I'd like to hear more about this brave young man a little later," said the big guy, "but in the mean time tell me what you learned about Evail Elderberry. Did you ever see him?"

"I did see him, on three separate occasions. He's a dreadful looking fellow. He's all stooped over, and each time I saw him he was wearing a mean and hateful-looking scowl on his face. It looks as though he's angry at everyone he sees. And he's as bald as a Genpuni egg," Mandy laughed in spite of herself, "and has a terrible, high pitched, raspy voice like he always has a sore throat. I'm quite sure that he couldn't sing a lick."

Santa shared her laugh, and she continued. "The grumpy old Elf can sure yell, though! He tried for days to shout louder than the music that was playing over the loud speakers. Everybody just ignored him, though, and danced in the streets. After a few days he finally gave up; much to our delight." Mandy sighed as she suddenly felt a pang of consciousness. "I don't mean to speak

74

evil of him, Santa. Actually, I felt sorry for him. I mean, after all, he was born with mischiefitus."

"Excellent," replied Santa, "it does my heart good to see that you feel empathy toward the old Elf, but please understand that mischiefitus is not an incurable condition. One must have the desire to be cured, as you did, Mandy. That desire entered your heart the moment you realized what you had done when you set all the Genpuni free. Evail Elderberry was born with mischiefitus, but he's never had the desire to be free of the condition. Even after many seasons of my doing everything I knew to do for him, he still refused to be willing to turn from his evil ways. At that point it was clear that he had made his choice, and the person he is today is due to his own choice."

Santa looked over his glasses at Mandy as though he were asking if she understood. "Yes, Santa, I understand; but I still feel sorry for him."

"I'm glad you do," Santa said softly. "As I told you before, I still have hope in my heart. I always will." The jolly old fellow nodded his approval of Mandy's attitude toward Evail Elderberry. "Now tell me, Mandy, how many Elves would you say are still loyal to their 'Emperor'"? Santa Claus used his hands to make quotation marks in the air to place emphasis on the word emperor.

"I don't think there are very many, Santa, but I can't say just how many." Then her voice lightened. "Not nearly as many as there once were, that's for sure. Almost all the guards who were sent into the streets to try to stop the celebrating traded their uniforms for regular clothes and joined the village people. Another thing, Santa, they're not called Elves down there; they're called Sleves."

Santa chuckled. "Yep, I've heard that before. It's a play on the spelling of Elves, the letters have been switched around."

Mandy laughed at this. "Why didn't I notice that before? That's funny. But it's sure not funny how they were treated down there…made to forget about where they came from, no mention of the Baby Jesus, or Christmas, or anything happy. And they were all forced to have the name Elderberry. Can you imagine, *Marko Elderberry*, that sounds crazy, doesn't it?"

Santa chuckled again. "That does sound odd, but then again, nothing that Evail Elderberry has done would surprise me very much."

The pair went on for another two hours with Mandy Mayflower telling Santa everything she could remember about the people of the South Pole: how they lived, how they worked, how they were punished at the hands of the guards, how they used dogs to pull their little sleighs, and how those in the good graces of the Emperor would chase and flog the poor hapless Penguins, simply for the fun of it.

"That's a disgrace!" Santa pounded his desktop with a sharp rap of his hand. "Those poor creatures can't even fly away."

"Just wait until you hear about the ice plains," replied Mandy, and then spent considerable time telling Santa about the perils of those who dared cross the Emperor or break his rules. "Isn't there something that can be done? You said you have a plan." Mandy's voice was pleading, filled with concern for the people she'd come to care about so deeply. Santa also knew that much of that concern was especially for Marko.

"Indeed I do have a plan, but first I want to hear more about this Marko fellow. It seems as though we owe him many thanks for protecting you and coming to your assistance." Santa smiled at Mandy's blush. "You have come to care for him, I see."

The girl's blush became full blown embarrassment, but still she managed a slight nod of the head. "He's such a nice boy, Santa, and if not for him I fear that I would have failed at my mission. And yes, Santa, I like him very much. When I left I promised him that I would see if there is anything you can do to get his family back here. I know I shouldn't ask, but...."

"You do like this young man, don't you?" Santa beamed at the thought of young love in the kingdom. "Let me tell you all about the plan I have that will go into effect the morning of Christmas Eve. I will travel to the South Pole with a full load of toys as well as gifts for the adults. I will teach them the true meaning of Christmas by telling them about the birth of the Baby Jesus, the importance of giving to one another, and the importance of love. Then I will invite all who wish, to move back to the North Pole. This separation has gone on much too long, and it's time for healing. I'm sure that every Elf in the kingdom will welcome back their long lost relatives and friends with open arms."

"Oh, Santa," cried Mandy, "that would surely make me very happy, and lots of other people, too!"

"Yes," Santa nodded, "but there is one thing that concerns me. It is you, Mandy, my dear sweet little Elf. It is a little more than a week before I can put my plan into action, and if your mischiefitus is completely cured during that time I fear you will not remember your trip to the South Pole."

Mandy stared at Santa; a puzzled look on her young and innocent face. Then she remembered her mother and Santa saying that she would would have no memory of her mischievous acts. What Santa was saying began to sink in.

"You may not remember any of the people you met there either, since everyone you met was through an act of mischief. I'm so sorry, Mandy. Had I known you would make such a great friend, I wouldn't have...."

"No, Santa, don't say that," snapped Mandy, cutting him off in mid-sentence. "This had to be done for the good of everyone, not just for Christmas, or us here at the North Pole, but for them too." Tears flooded her eyes. She knew Santa Claus was warning her that she might not have any memory of Marko. Even if Santa managed to get him back to the North Pole, he might be a stranger to her. Her head hung low, and Santa could hear the softness of her almost-silent sobs. Mandy's heart was breaking at the thought of losing her memories of her dear Marko. Suddenly she looked up with a firm determination in her eyes. "Santa," she declared, "I want to be cured of mischiefitus. I want to be free of ever being tempted to cause mischief again, but not at the expense of losing my memory of Marko. If I am forever known as Mandy the Mischievous Elf, then so be it. I will do my very best not to give in to temptations or cause any trouble for you, but Santa.....it's Marko." Again the girl sobbed; this time Santa's heart broke for her.

Santa Claus gathered the listless little Elf into his arms. He could feel her body tremble and he could hear her sobs. "That's a choice you are free to make, my dear," the big man softly said, "but should you make that choice be aware that you cannot return to your old job at the doll factory. I'm sorry but you will never be allowed back into any of the shops or factories. There's nothing I can do about it, Mandy, you would be the next Keeper of the Genpuni." Santa shrugged his shoulders as he studied the tear-filled eyes of his little Elf; much to his relief he saw no contempt in them.

"That's okay," Mandy shrugged her shoulders in return and gave him a little smile through her tears, "the Genpuni love me just like I am."

"And so do I," Santa reassured her with another hug. "So do I."

Chapter Twenty-three

Paddy glanced up when he heard his office door open. "Why, Mandy, you're back." Old Paddy stood, stretched his back, then delivered a big hug to the downcast-looking girl. "What's up with the sad face? I thought you'd be happy to be home, although I didn't expect you to show up here. I figured you would go back to your regular job."

"It looks like this is my regular job," stammered Mandy, as tears glistened in her eyes, and before she could stop herself she'd told everything to the elderly Elf.

Paddy had the unenviable reputation throughout the Kingdom of Claus of never putting much thought into anything; everyone assumed that is why he had been the Keeper of the Genpuni for as long as anyone could remember. The job simply did not require a high level of expertise. For that reason, Mandy was completely surprised by what he said next.

"Mandy, when I was a young man, just a little older than you are now, I was bold and adventurous. I would climb the mountains, explore the valleys, and ride the twinkling of the setting sun to all parts of the world. I didn't see anything wrong with what I did, and I certainly didn't mean any harm in it; nonetheless I broke a lot of rules. I met a young lady once in one of the foreign lands I visited. She was the same age as me and so, so pretty. Her name was Becky McBride; I'll never forget her flaming red hair and her eyes as green as emeralds. Because she was much shorter than everyone else in her village, they made fun of her and picked on her a lot. To escape the bullying the other young people dished out she spent a lot of time alone in the meadows and along the streams that ran through her valley. That's where we met; that's where I kept going back to visit her, and that's where we fell in love."

Mandy's eyes were about to pop out of her head, and her mouth hung open in disbelief of what she had just heard. She had never heard of anyone making contact with any other member of the human family that was not an

Elf....except Santa Claus himself. "Are you serious?" Mandy exclaimed. "Did you get in trouble?"

"Not really." Paddy shrugged his shoulders. "The boss wasn't very happy with me, of course, and he gave me this job forever. But before he gave me this job, he also gave me a choice."

"You had a choice," interrupted Mandy, "and you chose this?"

"No, I don't mean a choice of jobs. There was no way that Becky would've been allowed to come here, for that is strictly against the rules. She wouldn't have come here anyway. Here we have snow and ice all the time; but in Ireland, where she lived, there was hardly any snow and everything was lush and green most all the time. I had the choice to stay there with her."

Mandy's young and tender heart fluttered as she suddenly realized the importance of what Paddy was telling her. "Why didn't you stay?" Her words were barely audible as they caught in her throat.

"My family and friends convinced me that it would be the wrong thing to do." Old Paddy took a deep breath and let it out with a sigh. "A season passed before I realized what a terrible mistake I'd made; I spent another season searching for her. Becky never returned to the meadows, and I never saw her again. She gave up on me, but only after she believed I had given up on her. I'd made my choice and I've lived with it for all these generations."

Paddy made his way to the window and studied the few snowflakes that were drifting down from the graying skies. "I never married, you know, never had a family. That's not how I wanted things to be, mind you, but that was the results of my choice." After a full three minutes of silently staring out the window, Paddy turned to Mandy and spoke again. "Young lady, our choices have long-lasting effects. You say that you're willing to be bothered with the mischiefitus for the rest of your life in exchange for the memory of your friend. I admire your courage, but please be aware that you have no way of knowing what awaits you on the horizon. Think about this, and might I suggest a few prayers." Paddy's gloom faded with his final words, and his usual smile reappeared.

"I will," declared Mandy as she rushed across the room into the awaiting arms of the elderly Elf for a big hug, "I promise I will."

For the next several days Mandy fought the feeling of her mischiefitus leaving her. Her decision had been made; she thought endlessly of Marko and her time at the South Pole. She remembered every detail about Marko: the dimple in his cheek at the corner of his mouth that only appeared when he smiled, the unruly tuft of hair that she doubted he was aware of, and the little skip in his step that told of his happiness whenever they were together. Yes, she had made up her mind. Her memories she would keep, even if it meant she would be pestered by the mischiefitus all her days, and even if she, like her friend Paddy, would forever be the Genpuni keeper. Now with only two days left until Christmas Eve, and the big plan that Santa Claus would put into action, she felt like nothing could take her memories. But she was wrong.

Chapter Twenty-four

"Good morning, my favorite little troublemaker," said Paddy in a cheerful voice, "did you sleep well last night?"

"I did, thank you, Paddy," she replied. "I feel so rested this morning, and what a beautiful morning it is. Tomorrow is Christmas Eve; I'm so excited."

"I'll bet you are." Paddy playfully winked at Mandy. "I'll bet you're anxious to see Marko again." The older Elf reached out offering her a cup of hot chocolate.

"Who?" Mandy's puzzled expression caught Paddy completely off guard, and he dropped the cup of hot chocolate, shattering the mug and sending droplets of sticky cocoa in all directions.

"Oh, my dear!" he exclaimed. After cleaning up the mess, he rushed out the door without saying another word.

"That's odd," muttered Mandy as she watched the old Elf hobble as nimbly as he could toward the village center.

"She's cured, Santa," Paddy huffed and puffed, for he was short of breath after his brisk walk. "I mentioned Marko just now and she didn't have the foggiest idea who I was talking about. Yesterday she was walking on a cloud at the mention of his name, and now....nothing, she just looked at me like I'd lost my mind. I feel so sad for her. She tried so hard." Paddy finally fell into a nearby chair with a look of dread washing over him.

Santa shook his head, partly in disbelief, partly out of disappointment. "I was really hoping she could hold on," he said softly, "at least until the plan is completed. Then maybe things would have worked out for them. Now it will be like starting over, and who knows, the circumstances are totally different now." Santa Claus leaned back in his big chair. "Thank you for sharing this news with me, Paddy. At least now I can advise that young man before he gets such a huge shock. That is, if he chooses to return."

Chapter Twenty-five

Mandy Mayflower still weighed heavily on Santa's mind and heart as he made final preparations for his early morning trip to the South Pole. Although he was terribly distracted, Santa had managed to see that the additional load of special gifts for all the residents of that foreign land had been securely bagged and packed onto the sleigh. He would be off in a short while on the longest Christmas Eve flight he'd ever made.

"I'm sure, even before I ask, that all your preparations for the homecoming are done and we are ready to welcome our long lost relatives and friends back to the place where they belong?" Santa's inquiry was met with big smiles and nodding heads from Rocco Roundrock and Hollie Hoxlee. They were in charge of seeing that the returning Elves were made to feel welcome and comfortable in Santa's absence. He, himself, would not be back to the North Pole until very late in the night, or maybe not even until daybreak on Christmas Morning.

"Relax, Santa," assured Rocco, "everything has been taken care of. The Great Hall of Trees is decorated, and waiting. And might I say, Santa, that Cassie Carvanna has outdone herself once again. If you liked the big celebration we held a few months ago, you'll really like this one. Just hurry home so you won't miss it all."

"I'll be back as quickly as I can," answered Santa Claus as he climbed aboard his sleigh and caught a firm grip on the leather reins of his trusty team of reindeer. "But you know that this is something that cannot be rushed. There are times when I cross paths with someone who needs special attention." Santa nodded, and in turn Rocco nodded back. "Merry Christmas, my friends;" and with a click of his tongue, and a flick of the reins, he was off like a flash, leaving only the jingling of the harness bells on his wake. The crowd of Elves that always came together on this special day to watch Santa

take off on Christmas Eve cheered and wished him Merry Christmas, a safe journey, and God speed.

Like a streak, Santa raced through the atmosphere at incomprehensible speeds, and soon he was nearing his destination. The South Pole, in all its beauty, is still a harsh and inhospitable place for anything or anyone who requires warmth and shelter. Somehow, though, the Elves had managed to survive, and even multiply. Santa had put much thought into bringing the Elves home; once he knew it was time he never faltered in his decision. He thought he was ready to greet them, to welcome them back into the family, to celebrate Christmas with them. All of Santa's pondering and wondering, however, could not prepare him for what he was in store for.

Santa landed on the main street of the village of Elderberryville to a silent and orderly crowd who at once fell to their knees and bowed their heads, as if in worship. Beyond, Santa could see a makeshift Christmas Tree constructed of sticks and wire, and a dozen other available materials and decorated with an array of homemade ornaments and tinsel. On top of the tree sat a likeness of the jolly old fellow himself. Had Santa not been so puzzled and confused over his reception, he might have laughed at the little statue, for it was much too slender. But his eyes did not linger on the tree very long, they quickly returned to the silent and humble figures before him.

There were no Christmas Carols playing over the loud speaker system as he thought there would be. Following weeks of desperate attempts to stop the music, Evail Elderberry had finally succeeded. In the process, however, he had destroyed all of his computer equipment. Thankfully, all the village people had received word of Santa's arrival, and his intentions. Apparently someone had written down the words to some of the carols, obviously adjusting them to fit their needs; for at that moment they burst into song.

"Joy to the world for Santa has come. Let us receive our king, let every heart....."

And suddenly it was clear to Santa what was happening here, "Stop!" he bellowed, holding up his hands. Santa Claus had realized these poor, downtrodden Elves were seeing him as something he was not. "Stop singing, and please stand up."

Slowly everyone stood. "But, Santa Claus, you are most powerful; should we not bow down to you?" One brave young man dared to asked.

"I am *not* most powerful, and you should *never* bow down to me," declared Santa.

"But, Santa, you are powerful enough to banish us to this place," continued the young man, "does that not make you most powerful?"

Santa hopped down from his sleigh as to not tower above his people so, and rested his hands upon the shoulders of the young man who had dared speak. "I banished only one Elf to this place. The rest of you are here because of choices that were made by your forefathers." Then, for the next while, Santa told the whole story to the Elves of the South Pole. He told them the truth about Evail Elderberry and about how he had deceived and bullied some of his friends and family into following him to this remote place. And he told them the truth about Christmas; about a loving God and the greatest gift that had ever been given, when He allowed His Son to be born among men, as a light to a dark and sinful world, and a pathway to forgiveness. "Yes," said Santa, "it is time for forgiveness and it is time for you all to be reunited with your loved ones." Then Santa returned to his sleigh and produced a glittering star. He made his way through the crowd to the Christmas Tree and promptly replaced the figure on top with the star. With their new knowledge of Christmas and the story of the birth of Baby Jesus in their minds, the gathering cheered their approval.

"Now I must see two people," declared Santa, "Marko Elderberry and Evail Elderberry."

Marko immediately stepped forward receiving Santa's hand in a firm and friendly handshake. "Marko, you have proven yourself a trustworthy and loyal friend, and I have chosen you to lead this journey home. But first I must speak with you in private concerning your friend, Mandy."

A look of anticipation came over Marko's face as he took Santa by the elbow and led him to a quiet place. There Santa explained every detail of Mandy's condition to the saddened young man. His chin came to rest on his chest at the news of her having no memory of him.

"I know you have feelings for Mandy, and I know she had those same feelings for you, but this will be like starting over as far as she's concerned. Mandy is a good girl, Marko, she has a heart as big as the sky. Although the circumstances will be different, I can't help but believe that she will befriend you and show you the same kindness that you showed her when she first arrived here."

Marko nodded his head in acceptance of leading the journey home and the challenge of winning Mandy's heart once again. Santa then instructed him on how to prepare the others for their travels.

Back among the villagers at the Christmas Tree, there was a great celebration with Santa handing out gifts to young and old as he laughed and relayed well wishes from family members a world away. The joy of giving rang throughout the village and went on for a long time before someone spotted the Emperor lurking in the shadows of the village houses. The crowd fell silent and all turned to glare at their former, misguided leader. Once again Santa made his way through the gathering and approached Evail Elderberry.

"You wanted to see me, Santa Claus?" His voice was squeaky and nasally, his posture terrible. His rounded, stooped back told Santa that this place had indeed not been kind to the old Elf.

"Evail," Santa extended his hand, which was not well received. "I have come to take these people home." Santa hesitated a few seconds before he spoke again. "I make this offer to you also if you will turn from your evil ways."

Evail Elderberry's hard stare slowly softened and his head slowly drooped forward. "No, Santa," he shook his head from side to side, "it's too late for me. I had my chance and didn't take it. Take these people back to the North Pole where they belong; I will live out my last days, alone, in this horrible place that I deserve. Not one Elf stands with me now, that's the way it should have been all along. I realized my mistake soon after I got here, but my pride and unwillingness to ask forgiveness wouldn't allow me to say so. I let my stubbornness consume me; but believe me, Santa, I know how wrong I have been all along." Evail took a deep breath and let it out slowly. "Safe travels to you all," he called out before turning to go.

"Evail," Santa spoke loudly enough for all to hear, "even though you never asked, I have *always* forgiven you."

Evail Elderberry stopped for a few seconds but did not turn around, fearing that others might see the tears in his clouded old eyes.

Chapter Twenty-six

Later that night, following a successful journey on the Sun's Twinkle, the long lost, and in some cases the long forgotten about, Elves of the South Pole were welcomed back home with open arms and a grand celebration. All the Elves were introduced to their families, their family names were restored, and instantly bonds were made and old friendships rekindled. Not one single person was objectionable; all wrongs were forgiven, and all was well in the Kingdom of Claus. Even the well concealed Elf Tripper shyly emerged from his hiding place and rejoined his ancestral family: the Tanglewood's.

Although Santa had instructed Rocco not to make too big of a deal about Mandy Mayflower's part in all of this, it almost took on a life of its own. Scores of happy and joyful Elves, from both Poles, approached her to thank her for what she had done to bring their population back together. Mostly she just smiled and nodded. Santa had told her all about the recent adventure she'd been on, and although she could not remember it, she sensed that she had met these people before; one in particular…a handsome young lad, with twinkling eyes and a smile that could light up a dark room. Out of curiosity she kept watching his movements and on several occasions caught his return glance.

"Who is that young man?" Mandy dared ask Hollie Hoxlee as the two ladies stole away to a quieter corner sipping their hot chocolate.

"That's Marko," replied Hollie, "he was their leader during their journey home."

"*Leader*," exclaimed Mandy, "but he's so young."

"Young, yes," answered Hollie, "but also smart and brave." Hollie then smiled and slipped away into a small crowd of merrymakers, leaving Mandy to ponder on her wondering of this handsome young man.

The homecoming celebration went on all night with much laughter and joy. The newcomers were treated to foods and drinks they had never heard of, much less tasted. Even the older Elves like GG had long forgotten the taste of hot chocolate or the feel of a marshmallow on their tongues. A bland and dreary life they had lived, and at present it was fresh in their minds, making it easy and only natural to resolve that they would never, ever be separated from their home again.

Shortly after the sun cast its first warming rays of the new day over the village, Santa Claus made his return. It was Christmas Day; his work was done for yet another season. Climbing down from his sleigh Santa looked to the East; a brilliant blue was chasing away the reds and pinks and purples of the dawn, and he was struck by it's beauty. He paused to thank God for all the blessings he'd been given and once again promise to always stand firm on the side of goodness. Christmas had not been disrupted; Elves that had been separated from their homeland for generations had returned home, and Mandy Mayflower had been cured. Just then a thought occurred to him that brought on a big smile and he said out loud, "and I don't have to worry about any mischiefitus popping up, not unless Mandy has a third daughter anyway."

Unfortunately the jolly old fellow's contemplations were interrupted much too soon as he was shuffled off by attendants to join the Christmas Celebration, which lasted well into the afternoon.

Chapter Twenty-seven

Much needed to be done during the days following the homecoming. With the addition of so many new residents, new cottages had to be built, and in some cases new streets and lanes had to be cleared. Some houses that were abandoned when their occupants followed Evail Elderberry still stood empty and in a state of disrepair. Everyone pitched in to help; not one task lay idle very long before some willing Elf gladly took it up. Santa could see that soon everyone's needs would be taken care of. Of course he had to make sure everybody had a job. With Rocco's help, however, he soon had almost all that worked out.

On New Year's Day, Hollie Hoxlee announced that she and her long time fiance, Harvey Halltree, would wed in the spring. With this announcement, she submitted a request that Santa assign her a new position, one more suitable for a young bride. This left him without an assistant to his assistant, but it also provided an answer to a question that had had him somewhat baffled: what to do with Marko. So, just like that, Rocco Roundrock had a new assistant. Santa Claus was well pleased to learn that Marko was willing to accept the position. Of course this meant that he would have to undergo an extensive training program, for he would need to be very familiar with all the workings of the kingdom, and capable of fulfilling any duty assigned to him.

Two weeks later, Mandy jumped at the creaking of the opening door and the sound of Santa's happily, booming voice. She had been hand-feeding the Genpuni, softly speaking to them as if they were themselves people, and listening to the subtle changes of their cooing as they returned the love and affection that they were being given. Not expecting visitors, she whirled around in time to see Santa and the handsome young man she'd briefly met at the homecoming, smiling at her startled expression.

"Mandy, my dear, since you insist on staying here at the hutches as the

Genpuni keeper I have another job for you," said Santa through his smile. "This is Marko Mainsail, I'm sure you've met him, have you not?" Mandy's blush told that she had and prompted Santa to continue. "As you know, Hollie is getting married and has asked for a new position. I have placed Marko in that vacant position, however, he needs a lot of training. I thought this might be a good place to start. A few weeks with you and he will be well-versed in the care of the Genpuni. Marko, this young lady is Mandy Mayflower." Santa could see the surprise and the look of doubt in her eyes, after all, Paddy had retired only a few short days ago. "You'll do just fine," he assured her, patted her on the head as he often did, and then departed.

For a few seconds Mandy studied the face of the young man who looked at her as if he already knew her. Marko Mainsail, she thought, that's a nice name. "My name is Mandy," she reached out to shake his hand.

"My name is Marko," he replied, taking her hand in a firm but gentle grip.

"Marko, this is the Genpuni Hutch; these are the Genpuni," she turned to introduce him to the flock of birds who were watching the couple as if they understood the meaning of all this. "As you can see, this is not the cleanest job you could have." The birds cooed loudly, bobbed their heads, and flapped their wings in protest of her assessment, and the young couple laughed.

Marko's eyes twinkled like stars, and his heart fluttered like the wings of the Genpuni to see her happy and hear her laughter again. "Mandy, I used to work at the fish house; dirty jobs don't scare me." They both laughed again, and just like that the friendship that Marko had so hoped could be found again, blossomed before his very eyes.

And so goes it, the story of Mandy, The Mischievous Elf.

Here are
some coloring
pages so you
can have fun
coloring Mandy
all different
colors.